TAKE IT EASY
American Idioms

Pamela McPartland
Hunter College
City University of New York

Illustrations by **Alexander Kaletski**

 Prentice Hall Regents, Englewood Cliffs, NJ 07632

Library of Congress Cataloging in Publication Data

McPartland, Pamela.
   Take it easy.

     1. English language—Text-books for foreigners.
2. English language—Idioms, corrections, errors.
3. English language—Conversation and phrase books.
4. English language—Terms and phrases. I. Title.
[PE1128.M327]   428.3'4   80-25142
ISBN 0-13-882902-0

to my mother Rosie

Printed in the United States of America

20 19 18 17

Editorial/production supervision and
  interior design by Marybeth Brande
Front cover design by Alexander Kaletski
Manufacturing buyer: Harry P. Baisley

PRENTICE-HALL INTERNATIONAL, INC. *London*
PRENTICE-HALL of AUSTRALIA PTY. LIMITED, *Sydney*
PRENTICE-HALL of CANADA, LTD., *Toronto*
PRENTICE-HALL of INDIA PRIVATE LIMITED, *New Delhi*
PRENTICE-HALL of JAPAN, INC., *Tokyo*
PRENTICE-HALL OF SOUTHEAST ASIA PTE. LTD., *Singapore*
WHITEHALL BOOKS LIMITED, WELLINGTON, *New Zealand*

Contents

Acknowledgments

I wish to express my appreciation to the many people who contributed directly or indirectly to this book. First, I would like to thank Dr. Margaret Bedard of the College of New Rochelle, Professor John Fanselow and Professor Clifford Hill of Teachers College, Columbia University. I am especially indebted to Mr. Charles Barbosa who sparked my interest in idioms, and to my colleagues, Alan Devenish, Harriet Rubin, Joseph Barbarino, Robert Fertitta and Susan Schevers for testing out various drafts of the material in their classes, and making invaluable suggestions. The people who deserve much of the credit for this book are all the students who responded so well to the material, particularly Debora Tavares, Felix Bryla, Kazuo and Mieko Yamane, Mario and Doris Ponce, Angelica Sarmiento, Margret Dunkel, Bernard Yearly, Hiroko Fuse and Takashi Misu.

Richard Grassey, formerly of Prentice-Hall was the one who got the ball rolling, and Pam Kirshen, of Prentice-Hall contributed guidance and many suggestions for improving the book.

A special word of thanks goes to Alexander Kaletski whose insight and imagination played a major part in shaping the book into its present form.

Pamela McPartland
February 19, 1980

To the Student

Take It Easy is a book about idioms. In fact, "take it easy" is an idiom. An idiom is a group of words (two or more) which together form a unit. The meaning of the unit is different from the meaning of each of the individual words. For example, the group of words "take it easy" means "relax." The word, "take," alone, does not mean "relax," and "easy," alone, does not mean "relax," but when they are combined, as in "take it easy," they form a unit which means "relax."

This does not mean that every group of words is an idiom. For example: "in the morning," and "on the desk," are groups of words but they do not form a unit of meaning. Therefore, they are not idioms.

Many words used in English idioms come from Old English (Anglo-Saxon), or Middle English, ancestors of the English we use today. Their one-word equivalents often come from Latin. For example:

$$\begin{array}{ccc} \text{talk into} & = & \text{convince} \\ \text{Old English} & & \text{Latin} \end{array}$$

Therefore, idioms are at the heart of the English language. As you probably have noticed, idioms sound less formal than their Latin equivalents. For example:

She *made up* an excuse.   (informal)
She *invented* an excuse.   (formal)

This does not mean that all idioms are slang or incorrect English. Most idioms are perfectly acceptable forms of expression and appear in literature, magazine and newspaper articles, and can be heard in speeches, and radio and television broadcasts.

By doing the exercises in this book, you will learn to recognize and use 164 verb idioms. First, you will read an introductory passage which contains several idioms related to one theme. Each theme is practical and should help you communicate better in your everyday life. Then, you will do exercises to discover the meaning of the idiom, and to learn the position of any objects that the idiom requires. For example:

get [   ] across

He got _____ across _____. (it)
　　　　　a　　　　　　 b

In the text, the position of the object is shown by brackets, [   ].

But to use idioms correctly, it is not enough to know the meaning and the position of the object. You must also know what words are generally associated with each idiom.
For example:

Put on _____.

    a.　(X) your glasses
    b.　(X) your necklace
    c.　( ) your comb and brush

Both a and b can used with the idiom *put on,* but c cannot.

This book has special listening comprehension exercises and tapes to give you practice hearing the idioms in context. This also serves as excellent preparation for the Listening Comprehension section of the T.O.E.F.L. (Test of English as a Foreign Language).

To master idioms, you must also practice using them in your own sentences. There are Practical Application exercises to give you the opportunity to write original sentences using the idioms. You will also find exercises which focus on the *preposition or **particle which follows the verb in many idioms.

*A preposition is a word which follows a verb and requires an object.
Examples: He escaped *from* prison. We are leaving *for* Chicago.
**A particle is a word that is used with a verb to give the verb a special meaning. A particle is not followed by an object.
Examples: We must get *together.*　　Go *ahead.*

For example:

I can't cope _____ this situation any longer. You are driving me _____ of my mind. You know it gets _____ my nerves, but you continue to do it anyway.

At the end of the book there is an extensive review section which tests all the idioms presented in the book. You will also find the following:

a. List of prepositions and particles
b. Idioms and the position of their pronoun objects and noun objects
c. Idioms listed according to preposition or particle
d. Alphabetical listing of the idioms
e. Transcripts of the listening comprehension exercises
f. Answer key

Take It Easy is designed for use in class but it may also be used for self study since the answers are given in the book. The important thing is to take it easy! Don't try to memorize each idiom. By doing all the exercises you will learn more and more about how to use each idiom. The study of idioms can be enjoyable as well as rewarding. Idioms are at the heart of English and they will bring you closer to a native-like command of the English language.

To the Teacher

Take It Easy is a book of verb idioms. It contains ten lessons with idioms presented in a variety of contexts including a dialog, monolog, resume, letter, advertisement, etc.

Take It Easy is the first book of idiomatic expressions to present idioms relating to a specific topic (e.g. work, love, travel) in a meaningful context *and* provide extensive exercises to help students gain mastery of the idioms.

The material is geared to high intermediate or advanced students of English as a second or foreign language. By the time students reach the advanced level they recognize the importance of being able to understand and use idiomatic English.

There are varying degrees of idomaticity, that is, some idioms are considered highly idiomatic (e.g. come up with, have a crush on) and others are considered semi-idioms (e.g. cope with, apply for). If, for example we removed or changed any of the words in the idiom *come up with,* we would not retain the meaning, i.e., come with, come up, go up with, come, do not mean 'invent.' However, with the idiom *cope with,* we can eliminate the preposition *with,* or change *cope* to *deal* and still retain the meaning of the idiom, that is, 'tolerate.'

come up with	≠	come with, come up, go up with, come
cope with	=	cope, deal with

Degrees of Idiomaticity

Semi-idioms_____True idioms

cope with	come up with
apply for	have a crush on
turn around	drop by
listen to	cut out
fill up	run over

Idioms have been given a variety of names including: two-word verbs; phrasal verbs; prepositional verbs; and idomatic expressions. For the sake of simplicity, all the expressions in this text will be referred to as *idioms*.

Most of the idioms in **Take It Easy** fall into one of six patterns. The patterns are not presented in the text proper because it is not necessary for students to be able to discuss the patterns in order to learn the idioms. The danger in presenting the patterns to students is that they will be so pre-occupied with the patterns and the terms of each pattern that they will never fully grasp the meaning of the idiom itself. In the text, the students are simply shown the position of the direct object and/or prepositional object by the use of brackets, [   ].

The six patterns are: *Examples*

1. Intransitive verb + Particle	_ _	come on
2. Intransitive verb + Preposition	_ _ [ ]	cut across [the park]
3. Intransitive verb + Particle + Preposition	_ _ _ _ [ ]	go back to [his country]
4. Transitive verb + Particle	_ [ ] _	fill [it] up
5. Transitive verb + Preposition	_ [ ] _ [ ]	talk [him] into [it]
6. Transitive verb + Particle + Preposition	_ [ ] _ _ [ ]	drive [her] out of [her mind]

If a teacher wishes to present these patterns to the students, it would be necessary to clarify the following terms:

a. Intransitive verb = a verb which is not followed by an object. Examples of intransitive verbs: come, go, get, stay.
b. Transitive verb = a verb which must be followed by an object. Example: put [it] on. The object is *it*.
c. Particle = a word that is used with a verb to give special meaning to the verb. It is not followed by an object. Example: away, back.
d. Preposition = a word which follows a verb and requires an object. Example: from, of.

Note that some verbs can be both transitive and intransitive.

It should also be noted that some words function only as prepositions, some only as particles, and others as both prepositions and particles. (Refer to the Table of Prepositions and Particles.)

In addition to the above patterns this text includes complex expressions which contain other parts of speech besides prepositions and particles such as nouns and adjectives, examples: make *a living* by, drive somebody out of *his mind.* Many of these expressions although they look different fit into the above patterns.

Make [a living] by [   ] = Number 5, Transitive verb + Preposition

Drive [somebody] out of [his mind] = Number 6 Transitive verb +
Particle + Preposition

This book contains a few idioms which have a preposition or particle but do not fit into the above patterns, example:

bring [   ] into [contact] with [   ] = Transitive verb + Preposition +
Preposition

There are also a few idioms that have no preposition or particle and therefore do not fit into the patterns, example:

take it easy, make good time

Rather than concentrating on the grammatical patterns, the teacher may wish to spend class time helping students learn how flexible each idiom is, for example:

a. what tenses are commonly associated with the idiom
b. what grammatical structures are usually associated with the idiom, for example: passive voice, imperative form, the -ing form of the verb
c. what objects, in addition to those presented, are appropriate to the idiom
d. whether any words may be omitted without destroying the unit, example: *She winds him around her little finger.* "Little" may be omitted.
e. What pronouns are used with certain idioms, example: He drives *me* out of *my* mind, (Object pronoun and possessive pronoun)
She buried *herself* in *her* work, (Reflexive pronoun and possessive pronoun)
f. Which idioms are semi-idioms, i.e. which ones retain the meaning without the preposition. Examples: We couldn't *cope with* it. We couldn't *cope*
g. Other meanings of the idiom

All the idioms in *Take It Easy* are listed in their base form, i.e. the infinitive without "to" except those which contain a verb restricted to a certain form, examples:

xi

> *It stands* to reason   (Always third person singular)
> *To tell* you the truth   (Always the full infinitive)

Likewise, if the idiom contains a noun that is always either singular or plural, it is listed that way, example:

> go through the proper channel*s*

The idioms that appear in this text were chosen because of the frequency with which they are used in everyday life. The topics are among the most commonly discussed themes and they appear regularly in newspaper and magazine article. Certain idioms are labeled "informal" e.g. *calm down* and *fix up* because they have a casual tone and represent a closeness or familiarity between speakers. It also means that they are predominantly used in spoken rather than written English. There is no slang in this book because of its tendency to go out of date quickly.

Take It Easy uses an inductive approach to the study of idioms. Students read a story containing the idioms without seeing any definitions, and are then expected to guess the meaning of each idiom. The book does not contain mechanical drills which students can do by simply following a model. Each exercise requires the student to think, to draw his own conclusions about the idioms, and to guess.

Take It Easy can be used for a separate class in idioms or as an ancillary text for a grammar class, (e.g. idioms are fun to use to review the tenses) or for a vocabulary class or a conversation class. This material also provides excellent practice for the listening comprehension section of the TOEFL.

There are many ways to use this text. The number of different things that can be done to help students master the material depends, of course, on how much class time can be devoted to idioms. To complete the ten lessons in this book requires approximately twenty hours of class time. If that much time cannot be spent on idioms, it is recommended that only five chapters be covered a semester, or the students can be assigned most of the exercises for homework, except for the listening comprehension. If it is possible to spend more than twenty hours on this material, the students should be given a great deal of oral and written practice using the idioms in the students' own sentences and situations. The following suggestions are provided to help the teacher make good use of the exercises in the book:

I.   *THE ILLUSTRATIONS* help the students focus on the topic and remember particular idioms. The pictures generally do not illustrate the introductory passage but are related in a broad sense.

a.   The students describe the picture in their own words, as a pre-test. This can be an oral or written exercise.

b.   After they do exercises in the chapter, they can write their own story about the picture using as many idioms as possible.

xii

c. After covering two or three chapters, the students select one picture and ask each other questions about the idioms in those chapters. (There is an example of this in the review section at the back of the book.)

II. *THE INTRODUCTORY PASSAGE*
    a. The teacher reads the story aloud, then students retell it in their own words. This is the first step in guessing the meaning of the idioms from the context.
    b. The students read the passage line-by-line replacing each idiom with other words. Again, they are guessing the meaning.
    c. The students read each line and write the meaning on their 'Notes' page.
    d. The teacher or a student dictates the passage and the students write it below the illustrations.
    e. The students transform the story into a different tense, indirect speech, questions, etc.

III. *NOTES*
This page gives valuable information about grammar, style and the position of the object.
    a. The students write the meaning of the idiom.
    b. The students write sample sentences.
    c. The students copy sentences containing the idiom from a short story, novel, newspaper or magazine.
    d. The students give examples of appropriate direct objects and objects of the preposition for each idiom that requires an object.
    e. The students practice saying the idioms with correct stress. In general, prepositions are unstressed, and verbs and particles are stressed.

IV. *DEFINITIONS*
    a. After the students do this exercise, the teacher says a sentence using the meaning of the idiom and the students must say the sentence with the idiom. Students may wish to look at the list of idioms on the 'Notes' page.

V. *WORD ASSOCIATION*
a. The students must explain why one response is wrong. Some reasons are as follows:
    1. The answer repeats the meaning of the idiom
    2. There is a word missing
    3. It is a literal understanding of the idiom

4. The object must be:
   a. a person, or persons   b. a thing
   c. a situation   d. a place
   e. an action
   f. a specific thing, e.g. a country, an expensive item, a ruler, something negative, a problem
5. The grammar is incorrect, e.g. the idiom must be followed by the -ing form
6. It doesn't make sense (or it conflicts with the meaning of the idiom)
7. It is too general
8. It doesn't correspond to the subject

VI. *POSITION OF THE OBJECT*

a. The students change pronoun objects to nouns noting which idioms have two positions for the noun, e.g.,

> He built it up
> He built the company.
> He built the company up.

but

> We came across it.
> We came across an interesting advertisement.

VII. *LISTENING COMPREHENSION* This is a test of the students' ability to hear and understand the idioms when they are mixed with other words which may or may not be familiar to the student.
   a. The students discuss why two responses are incorrect. They will have to refer to the transcript.
   b. The students read and act out the dialogues adding their own sentences.

VIII. *FILL IN.* This is a review of the prepositions and particles in the idioms.

IX. *PRACTICAL APPLICATION* exercises give the students a chance to write original sentences containing the idioms by making use of the information given. These exercises can be done individually or in groups.
   a. The students discuss the topic after doing the exercise.

Remember, the important thing is to take it easy. It is difficult for students to learn precisely how to use each idiom in one course. This takes constant practice and reinforcement. However, by doing the exercises in this book, students will come very close to the mastery of 164 idioms.

CONVERSATION

Conversation

INTRODUCTORY PASSAGE

She: Excuse me, I usually don't **strike up** a conversation with strangers, but can you tell me what kind of dog that is? I've never seen one like that before.

He: It's a bull terrier. I **gather from** your accent that you're not American, but you speak English very well!

She: Thanks. **To tell you the truth,** I still have trouble with English, especially vocabulary.

He: It's funny, I was just reading an article about the English language. Can I **tell** you **about** it?

She: Sure. **Go ahead.**

He: It says that an educated adult has a vocabulary of about 250,000 words. And **listen to** this—English has more words than any other language; there are about 450,000 words in the dictionary!

She: Oh, **come on.** That's impossible.

He: I'm not **making** it **up.** It's right here in the paper.

She: Well, now I understand why it's difficult for me to express myself.

He: I think you are able to **get** your ideas **across** very well.

She: Yes, but when people ask me the simplest things, sometimes I just **clam up.**

He: You've **touched on** an interesting point. In the article, it says that the everyday words in English come from Anglo-Saxon, but the sophisticated words come from Latin. If your language comes from Latin, **it stands to reason** that it would be easier for you to discuss politics than to discuss everyday life.

She: I'm very sorry but I completely **disagree with** your theory.

He: Well, now that we aren't strangers anymore, perhaps I could **talk** you **into** continuing this conversation over dinner!

She: Okay, but no politics, please.

NOTES

*IDIOMS AND THE POSITION
OF THEIR OBJECTS*   *GRAMMATICAL NOTES   STYLE*

1. strike up   [   ] _____ object is usually a noun _____

_____

2. gather from   [   ]_____ object is usually a noun _____

_____   _____

3. to te.   [you]   [the truth] _____

_____   _____

4. tell   [   ]   bout   [   ] _____

_____

5. go ahead _____

_____

6. listen to   [   ] _____   _____

_____

7. come on _____ imperative form only _____

_____

8. make   [   ]   up _____

_____

9. get   [   ]   across _____

_____

10. clam up _____ informal

_____

11. touch on   [   ]   _____

_____

12. it stands to   [reason]   _____ informal

_____

13. disagree with   [   ]   _____

_____

14. talk   [   ]   into   [   ]   object of the prep. is usually the *-ing* form

_____

Use this page for one or more of the following exercises:

- Write the meaning of the idiom.
- Write sample sentences.
- Look for the idioms in short stories, novels, newspapers, or magazines, and copy the sentences containing them.
- Give examples of appropriate direct objects or objects of the preposition for each idiom that requires an object.
- Practice saying the idioms with correct stress. In general, verbs and particles are stressed, but prepositions are unstressed.

I. DEFINITIONS

DIRECTIONS: Mark the answer that is the closest synonym for the italicized idioms.

1. He loves to talk and can *strike up* a conversation with anybody.

        a. (   ) begin
        b. (   ) end
        c. (   ) continue

2. I *gather from* your remark that you are angry.

    a. ( )   hear
    b. ( )   understand from
    c. ( )   ignore

3. *To tell you the truth,* we're starving.

    a. ( )   to be honest
    b. ( )   to explain why
    c. ( )   in other words

4. *Tell* us *about* your accident.

    a. ( )   forget about
    b. ( )   demonstrate
    c. ( )   describe

5. The construction will *go ahead* as planned.

    a. ( )   be stopped
    b. ( )   be delayed
    c. ( )   continue

6. He is very stubborn and won't *listen to* anybody.

    a. ( )   pay attention to
    b. ( )   speak with
    c. ( )   understand

7. Oh *come on,* Michael, we know you're over thirty!

    a. ( )   stop saying something that isn't true
    b. ( )   hurry
    c. ( )   come with us

8. She didn't want to go to the party so she *made up* a good excuse.

    a. ( )   asked for
    b. ( )   wrote
    c. ( )   invented

9. She was so upset that she couldn't *get* the message *across*.

        a. ( ) ask questions about
        b. (✓) communicate
        c. ( ) receive

10. The witness was so nervous that when the lawyer began to question him, he *clammed up*.

        a. (✓) wasn't able to communicate
        b. ( ) was shaking
        c. ( ) answered immediately

11. During the press conference, the President *touched on* the unemployment problem.

        a. ( ) discussed fully
        b. ( ) discussed briefly
        c. ( ) avoided

12. He was arrested for the murder because he looked like the killer. *It stands to reason* that he is angry.

        a. ( ) it is surprising
        b. ( ) he wanted to say
        c. ( ) it is to be expected

13. She *disagreed with* her sister about what to buy their mother for Christmas.

        a. ( ) took the advice of
        b. ( ) had a different opinion from
        c. ( ) asked

14. He wanted to buy a Cadillac but his son *talked* him *into* buying a Porsche.

        a. ( ) convinced
        b. ( ) asked
        c. ( ) told

II. WORD ASSOCIATION

DIRECTIONS: Two of the three choices below can be used with the idiom. Mark the *two* answers that can be used to complete each sentence correctly.

1. We thought they were going to strike up _____.

        a. (   ) each other
        b. (   ) a friendship
        c. (   ) a conversation

2. The boss said to go ahead _____.

        a. (   ) forward
        b. (   ) with the plan
        c. (   ) without delay

3. He told his wife about _____.

        a. (   ) the accident
        b. (   ) his experience
        c. (   ) the time

4. I gather from your _____ you are upset.

        a. (   ) expression
        b. (   ) broken heart
        c. (   ) comment

5. To tell you the truth, _____.

        a. (   ) I don't know what you are talking about
        b. (   ) it's true
        c. (   ) I'm twenty-five years old

6. What kind of _____ do you listen to?

        a. (   ) people
        b. (   ) advice
        c. (   ) word

7. Oh come on, you _____!

      a. ( ) must be kidding
      b. ( ) are telling the truth
      c. ( ) are joking

8. The _____ touched on her love life.

      a. ( ) article
      b. ( ) speaker
      c. ( ) advertisement

9. It is still difficult for him to get _____ across.

      a. ( ) important information
      b. ( ) the voice on the radio
      c. ( ) jokes

10. She probably made _____ up.

      a. ( ) the dress
      b. ( ) the whole thing
      c. ( ) the story

11. The _____ unexpectedly clammed up.

      a. ( ) message
      b. ( ) entertainer
      c. ( ) patient

12. The agent couldn't talk the young couple into _____.

      a. ( ) buying the house
      b. ( ) anything
      c. ( ) join

13. It stands to reason _____.

      a. ( ) he will be fired
      b. ( ) it is expected
      c. ( ) she will ask for a divorce

14.   Why do you always disagree with your _____?

        a. ( ) son
        b. ( ) boss
        c. ( ) opinion

III. THE POSITION OF THE OBJECT

DIRECTIONS: Fill in *one* of the blanks (a or b) in each sentence with the object given in parentheses. *Three* of the sentences do not have objects. For those sentences, do not write anything.

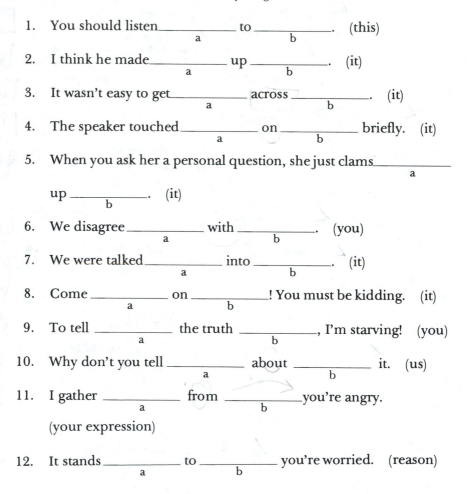

1.   You should listen_____ to _____. (this)
                    a   b

2.   I think he made_____ up _____. (it)
                    a   b

3.   It wasn't easy to get_____ across _____. (it)
                        a   b

4.   The speaker touched_____ on _____ briefly. (it)
                          a   b

5.   When you ask her a personal question, she just clams_____
                                               a

     up _____. (it)
          b

6.   We disagree_____ with _____. (you)
                 a   b

7.   We were talked_____ into _____. (it)
                  a   b

8.   Come _____ on _____! You must be kidding. (it)
              a   b

9.   To tell _____ the truth _____, I'm starving! (you)
                a   b

10. Why don't you tell _____ about _____ it. (us)
                    a   b

11. I gather _____ from _____you're angry.
                a   b
     (your expression)

12. It stands _____ to _____ you're worried. (reason)
               a   b

13. When one student is finished, the next should go_____
    a

    ahead _____. (it)
    b

14. She wanted to strike_____ up _____.
    a b

    (a conversation)

IV. LISTENING COMPREHENSION ANSWER SHEET

Part I

DIRECTIONS: You will hear a short dialogue followed by a question. After you hear each question, read the three choices and mark the response that answers the question correctly.

1. a. ( ) The woman always talks to other men.
   b. ( ) The woman couldn't find the restaurant.
   c. ( ) The woman started a conversation with a stranger.

2. a. ( ) The woman wants to see London, Rome, and Athens only.
   b. ( ) The woman prefers to see only one city.
   c. ( ) The woman wants to see everything in Europe.

3. a. ( ) The romance was coming along.
   b. ( ) The story wasn't true.
   c. ( ) He hadn't heard about it.

4. a. ( ) He listened to it.
   b. ( ) He turned off the tape recorder.
   c. ( ) It was difficult to hear.

5. a. ( ) He thinks it is better not to tell her the truth.
   b. ( ) It is serious.
   c. ( ) He really doesn't know if it is serious or not.

Part II

DIRECTIONS: You will hear a situation presented in one or two sentences. Listen to each statement and mark the response that most closely corresponds to the situation.

1. a. ( ) Arthur didn't become a member.
   b. ( ) Arthur joined the club.
   c. ( ) Arthur liked the facilities at the club.

2. a. ( ) Most of the interview was about her addiction to drugs.
   b. ( ) She didn't talk about her operation.
   c. ( ) She talked about her marriage.

3. a. ( ) Caroline's mother-in-law wants her to get a divorce.
   b. ( ) Caroline's mother-in-law wants her to stay married.
   c. ( ) Caroline is always fighting with her mother-in-law.

4. a. ( ) His parents named him Anthony Winston when he was born.
   b. ( ) He gave himself the name Winston.
   c. ( ) He gave himself the name Anthony.

5. a. ( ) He prefers to keep his tips secret.
   b. ( ) He reports all his income to the Internal Revenue Service.
   c. ( ) He reports his tips on his income tax form.

6. a. ( ) The victim was so nervous and afraid that she couldn't speak.
   b. ( ) The lawyer asked the robber many questions.
   c. ( ) The robber was nervous.

7. a. ( ) It is hard to make a choice because there are so many breeds.
   b. ( ) The choice is very limited.
   c. ( ) You must have a reason for buying a dog.

8. a. (   ) It is better to take as much time as necessary for each question.

    b. (   ) When you see a difficult question, don't even try to find the answer.

    c. (   ) It is better not to spend too much time on a difficult question.

9. a. (   ) Paul probably doesn't like war.

    b. (   ) Paul probably thinks war can be good.

    c. (   ) Paul likes all of Benjamin Franklin's sayings.

10. a. (   ) The travel agent said not to take a vacation in July, August, and September.

    b. (   ) The travel agent wanted to make it clear that it would be hot and humid during your vacation.

    c. (   ) The travel agent said it would be too hot for your dog.

V. FILL IN

DIRECTIONS: Fill in the blanks with the correct preposition or particle.

Man: I just overheard your conversation with that policeman.

I gather _____ your accent you are French.

1

Woman: Yes. _____ tell you the truth, I have been here only

2

three days.

Man: Well, I'm glad I decided to strike _____ a conversation

3

with you. Maybe I can tell you _____ the city.

4

Woman: Were you born here?

Man: No, but I spent most of my adult life here.

Woman: It stands _____ reason you know a lot about the city.

5

Man: Perhaps I could talk you _____ going for a ride on the
                                        6
ferry. I could show you the most important sights from there.

Woman: I'm sorry but I have a class in twenty minutes.

Man: Oh, come _____ !
                        7

Woman: I'm not making it _____ ; I'm really a student.
                                    8

Man: Listen _____ that—the ferry is leaving in two minutes.
                      9
It's a short ride, and besides, on the way I could teach you
how to get your ideas _____ in English. Practice is
                            10
much more important than sitting in a classroom.

Woman: I'm very sorry but I disagree _____ you. Anyway, I
                                              11
usually clam _____ when I'm with strangers for more
                  12
than a few minutes and . . . .

Man: You have touched _____ an interesting point. Maybe
                                13
you have trouble because you don't have enough practice
speaking with people.

Woman: That's not the point. If you had let me finish . . . .

Man: Oh I'm sorry. Please, go _____ .
                                        14

Woman: What I wanted to say was, I'm married.

Man: Big deal!

VI. PRACTICAL APPLICATION

Barbara Stevenson is being considered for the position of advertising director at a major company. After interviewing her, the personnel director wrote the following:

Barbara Stevenson

1. She expresses herself well.
2. She has a good imagination.
3. She is very friendly.
4. She doesn't like to talk about her previous job.
5. She is too easy with the people working for her.
6. She doesn't always answer the question.
7. She spends a lot of time talking about her children.
8. She proved that she knows everything about the advertising business. I recommend her for the job.

DIRECTIONS: Next to each idiom below, write a sentence using the information the personnel director wrote about Barbara Stevenson. Use the idiom in your sentence.

1. (get across) _____

    _____

2. (make up) _____

    _____

3. (strike up) _____

    _____

4. (touch on) _____

    _____

5. (disagree with) _____

    _____

6. (listen to) _____

_____

7. (tell about) _____

_____

8. (talk into) _____

_____

VII. ADDITIONAL EXERCISES

1. Make up a story about the picture at the beginning of the chapter. Use as many idioms as possible. This exercise can be written or oral.
2. Ask each other questions about the picture. You must use an idiom in your response.
3. Use the lines below the picture for a dictation exercise. The teacher or a student dictates the introductory passage and the students write it.
4. Rewrite the introductory passage in indirect speech.

2

WORK

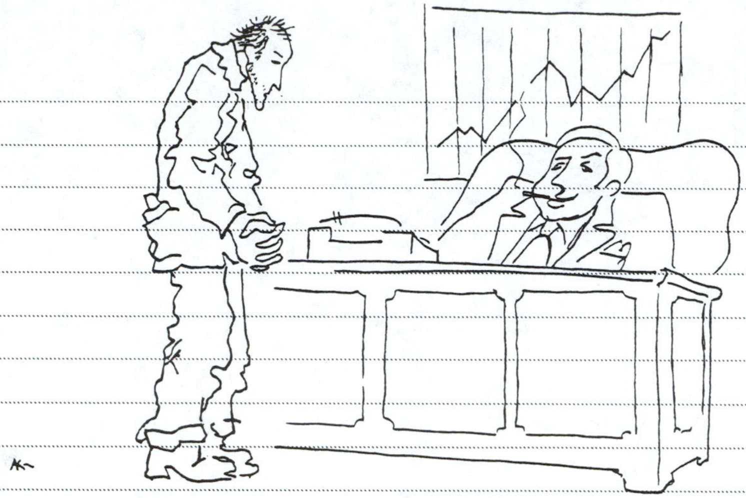

Work

INTRODUCTORY PASSAGE

Resumé

Raymond A. Kroc
Santa Barbara, California

WORK EXPERIENCE

1955–Present   Founder and Senior Chairman of the Board, McDonald's Corporation
I **made a deal with** the McDonald brothers in 1955. I wanted to use their name and the idea of their fast-food restaurant. I hoped to **cash in on** the need for good, inexpensive food served in a clean and pleasant atmosphere. Ten years later, I **bought** them **out** and they **signed over** the company to me. I continued to **build up** the business. To control the quality, all managers had to attend classes at the Hamburger University, which I helped **set up**. By 1980, McDonald's had **branched out** so quickly that there were 6,000 restaurants throughout the world. The company was **valued at** $4.6 billion. Now that can probably be **rounded off** to $5 billion.

1914–1955   Sales Manager, Lily Tulip Company
I sold Multimixers, which stirred six milkshakes at the same time. This job **brought** me **into contact with** hundreds of restaurant owners. Once I **arranged for** a meeting with Maurice and Richard McDonald, who had a busy restaurant in California. I wanted to **do business with** them. The meeting **paid off**. We **got down to** business and **entered into** a deal that made history.

Land Salesman, Florida
As a salesman I had to convince people to **invest in** land in Florida.

Jazz Pianist, Chicago, Illinois
For a few years, I **made a living by** playing piano. As a nightclub entertainer, I learned to **deal with** all types of people.

Ambulance Driver, Red Cross Ambulance Corps
During World War I, I **put in for** a position as an ambulance driver.

EDUCATION   Some high school

HONORS   American of the Year
AND   Golden Plate Award
AWARDS   Man of the Year

PERSONAL   Married; one child
                 Born October 5, 1902, in Chicago, Illinois
                 Interests: piano, baseball

Courtesy of the McDonald's Corporation, the fast-food chain.

NOTES

IDIOMS AND THE POSITION OF THEIR OBJECTS	GRAMMATICAL NOTES	STYLE
1. make [a deal] with [ ]		
2. cash in on [ ]		informal
3. buy [ ] out		
4. sign [ ] over		
5. build [ ] up		

6.   set   [   ]   up   _____

_____

7.   branch out   _____

_____

8.   value   [   ]   at   [   ]   _____ usually passive _____

_____

9.   round   [   ]   off   _____

_____

10.   bring   [   ]   into   [contact]   with   [   ]   _____

_____

11.   arrange for   [   ]   _____

_____

12.   do   [business]   with   [   ]   _____

_____

13.   pay off   _____ informal

_____

14.   get down to   [business]   _____

_____

15.   enter into   [   ]_____ object is usually a noun ___

_____

16.   invest in   [   ]   _____

_____

17.   make   [a living]   by   [   ]   _____ object is usually the -*ing* form

_____

18.   deal with   [   ]   _____

_____

19.   put in for   [   ]   _____

_____

Use this page for one or more of the following exercises:

- Write the meaning of the idiom.
- Write sample sentences.
- Look for the idioms in short stories, novels, newspapers, or magazines, and copy the sentences containing them.
- Give examples of appropriate direct objects or objects of the preposition for each idiom that requires an object.
- Practice saying the idioms with correct stress. In general, verbs and particles are stressed, but prepositions are unstressed.

I. DEFINITIONS

DIRECTIONS: Mark the answer that is the closest synonym for the italicized idioms.

1.   He *made a deal with* his client.

    a.   ( )   discussed it with
    b.   ( )   agreed to do business with
    c.   ( )   produced something with

2. Our competitor *cashed in on* the gas shortage.

        a. ( ) requested cash for
        b. ( ) ordered more because of
        c. ( ) benefited from

3. His partner *bought* him *out.*

        a. ( ) paid him for his share in the business.
        b. ( ) bought some additional shares in the company.
        c. ( ) sold everything to him.

4. She *signed over* the property to me.

        a. ( ) put her signature on the paper to confirm the sale or change in ownership
        b. ( ) leased
        c. ( ) wrote her name above my name to show that she bought the property from me.

5. In just two years the lawyer *built up* the firm.

        a. ( ) developed
        b. ( ) constructed
        c. ( ) renovated

6. The board of directors decided to *set up* a branch in Paris.

        a. ( ) keep
        b. ( ) establish
        c. ( ) increase the size of

7. The company *branched out* so fast that it went bankrupt.

        a. ( ) opened one branch
        b. ( ) increased its prices
        c. ( ) expanded in a new direction

8. The business was *valued at* half a million dollars.

        a. (   ) considered to be worth
        b. (   ) as expensive as
        c. (   ) sold for

9. She *rounded off* the total income to $7,500,000.

        a. (   ) added
        b. (   ) subtracted
        c. (   ) changed the total to a round figure

10. His job *brought* him *into contact with* a lot of artists.

        a. (   ) helped him meet
        b. (   ) helped him send letters to
        c. (   ) helped him call

11. Her secretary *arranged for* the conference.

        a. (   ) attended
        b. (   ) was responsible for planning
        c. (   ) cancelled

12. It was a pleasure to *do business with* that manufacturer.

        a. (   ) hire
        b. (   ) work for the same company as
        c. (   ) trade with or negotiate with

13. Her ingenious idea certainly *paid off.*

        a. (   ) succeeded
        b. (   ) cost a lot of money
        c. (   ) was free

14. After a few minutes of social talk, we *got down to business.*

        a. (   ) sat down
        b. (   ) talked about our jobs
        c. (   ) began to talk seriously

15. After discussing the deal for two weeks, the companies finally *entered into* negotiations.

> a. ( ) began
> b. ( ) finished
> c. ( ) considered

16. He made a mistake when he *invested in* those stocks.

> a. ( ) sold
> b. ( ) asked about
> c. ( ) bought and hoped to earn interest from

17. It was impossible for him to *make a living by* acting.

> a. ( ) support himself financially by
> b. ( ) live without
> c. ( ) have an interesting life by

18. As a salesman, he had to *deal with* the public.

> a. ( ) have contact with
> b. ( ) play cards with
> c. ( ) convince

19. After working for the company for three months, he *put in for* a promotion.

> a. ( ) rejected
> b. ( ) requested
> c. ( ) received

II. WORD ASSOCIATION

DIRECTIONS: Two of the three choices below can be used with the idiom. Mark the *two* answers that can be used to complete each sentence correctly.

1. Mr. Williams finally made a deal with _____.

> a. ( ) that client
> b. ( ) his enemy
> c. ( ) the new product

2.   _____ bought her out.

    a. ( ) One of her partners
    b. ( ) The man who had 100% of the stock
    c. ( ) A competitor

3.   She signed over _____ to me.

    a. ( ) the manager
    b. ( ) her share of the company
    c. ( ) the property

4.   He is the only person who could build up _____.

    a. ( ) the reputation
    b. ( ) the president
    c. ( ) the business

5.   _____ is branching out rapidly.

    a. ( ) The enterprise
    b. ( ) The office building
    c. ( ) The corporation

6.   _____ were valued at $100,000.

    a. ( ) The houses
    b. ( ) The estates
    c. ( ) The dollars

7.   Why don't you round off _____?

    a. ( ) the $50.00
    b. ( ) the figure
    c. ( ) the price

8.   I bet they are going to cash in on _____.

    a. ( ) the shortage
    b. ( ) the discovery
    c. ( ) the dollars

9. The president plans to set up _____.

        a. ( ) a new committee
        b. ( ) a central office
        c. ( ) an old library

10. _____ brought her into contact with many people.

        a. ( ) Her job
        b. ( ) Her trip
        c. ( ) Her nervousness

11. _____ arranged for his trip.

        a. ( ) His appointment
        b. ( ) His secretary
        c. ( ) The travel agent

12. We hope to do business with that _____.

        a. ( ) product
        b. ( ) supplier
        c. ( ) manufacturer

13. _____ finally paid off.

        a. ( ) Her creative ideas
        b. ( ) Buying those lottery tickets
        c. ( ) The bill

14. The two countries have decided to enter into _____.

        a. ( ) their old treaty
        b. ( ) negotiations
        c. ( ) a period of peace

15. They have invested all their money in _____.

        a. ( ) a Ferrari
        b. ( ) a stereo
        c. ( ) lunch

16. Because of his position, he has to deal with a lot of _____.

        a. ( ) business
        b. ( ) wholesalers
        c. ( ) companies

17. _____ got down to business within ten minutes.

        a. ( ) The executives
        b. ( ) The children
        c. ( ) The lawyer and his client

18. She has already put in for _____.

        a. ( ) a leave of absence
        b. ( ) a raise
        c. ( ) an application

19. It isn't easy to make a living by _____.

        a. ( ) studying
        b. ( ) working part-time
        c. ( ) selling magazines

III. THE POSITION OF THE OBJECT

DIRECTIONS: Fill in *one* of the blanks (a or b) in each sentence with the object given in parentheses. *Two* of the sentences do not have objects. For those sentences, do not write anything.

1. You should round _____ off _____ to the nearest
   a   b

   whole number.   (it)

2. He is going to cash in _____ on _____.   (it)
   a   b

3. It isn't easy to deal _____ with _____.   (them)
   a   b

4. She has already put in _____ for _____.   (it)
   a   b

5. It's hard to make a living _____ by _____.
          a   b

    (acting)

6. His position brought _____ into _____ contact
                    a   b

    with them.   (him)

7. He has arranged _____ for _____.   (it)
                a   b

8. You should have bought _____ out _____.   (him)
                    a   b

9. When everyone arrived we got down _____ to
                        a

    _____.   (business)
        b

10. The necklace was valued _____ at _____.   ($10,000)
                    a   b

11. They built _____ up _____.   (it)
            a   b

12. You should do business _____ with _____.   (them)
                    a   b

13. His idea didn't really pay _____ off _____.   (it)
                        a   b

14. They entered _____ into _____ too quickly. (it)
                a   b

15. The company has branched _____ out _____.   (it)
                        a   b

16. He didn't want to sign _____ over _____.   (it)
                    a   b

17. We want to make a deal _____ with _____.   (them)
                    a   b

18. He forgot to set _____ up _____.   (it)
                a   b

19. We are happy we invested _____ in _____.   (it)
                        a   b

IV. LISTENING COMPREHENSION ANSWER SHEET

DIRECTIONS: You will hear a situation presented in one or two sentences. Listen to each statement and mark the response that most closely corresponds to the situation.

1. a. ( ) She had to find a hotel herself.
    b. ( ) The airline found a hotel for her.
    c. ( ) The airline cancelled the flight because of the hotel.

2. a. ( ) The U.S. is a self-sufficient country.
    b. ( ) The U.S. trades with only European countries.
    c. ( ) The U.S. buys products from these countries and also sells products to them.

3. a. ( ) They talked too much and didn't do any work.
    b. ( ) They gossiped for a while and then began to work seriously.
    c. ( ) They did business with their friends.

4. a. ( ) Carnegie built many foundations with steel.
    b. ( ) Carnegie used his money to establish several foundations.
    c. ( ) Carnegie was a researcher.

5. a. ( ) He is unemployed now.
    b. ( ) He wants another job or more money at his present job.
    c. ( ) He got a raise.

6. a. ( ) The painting was sold for less than it was worth.
    b. ( ) The painting was worth $100,000.
    c. ( ) The painting was sold for $250,000.

7. a. ( ) He plays for free.
    b. ( ) He plays tennis for exercise.
    c. ( ) He is probably a professional tennis player.

8. a. ( ) He sold the entire company.

    b. ( ) He sold his share of the company.

    c. ( ) He asked his partner to lend him some cash.

9. a. ( ) The countries did business for five years.

    b. ( ) In five years they will trade with each other.

    c. ( ) They recently agreed to trade with each other.

10. a. ( ) The Standard Oil Company became so large that it was a monopoly.

    b. ( ) Rockefeller kept the company small.

    c. ( ) Rockefeller's company was average.

11. a. ( ) Finally, the applicant got less money.

    b. ( ) Finally, the applicant got more money.

    c. ( ) The proposed salary stayed the same.

12. a. ( ) The grandson received everything before the grandfather died.

    b. ( ) He left his grandson everything in his will.

    c. ( ) The grandfather signed everything he owned.

13. a. ( ) He worked with angry people in his office.

    b. ( ) He was angry all the time.

    c. ( ) He had to listen to complaints.

14. a. ( ) The strike wasn't settled.

    b. ( ) The strike lasted two weeks.

    c. ( ) The management gave the workers two-weeks' salary.

15. a. ( ) In 1970 the U.S. population was exactly 203,000,000.

    b. ( ) In 1970 the U.S. population was about 203,000,000.

    c. ( ) The U.S. population in 1917 was exactly 203,211,926.

16. a. ( )   His gadget wasn't successful.

    b. ( )   It was a good investment.

    c. ( )   He saved his money instead of investing it.

17. a. ( )   The Teamsters Union joined the largest labor union in the U.S.

    b. ( )   The Teamsters Union took him to see the largest union in the U.S.

    c. ( )   He met a lot of truck drivers through the Teamsters Union.

18. a. ( )   They thought about selling American products in Japan.

    b. ( )   They got rich by selling American products in Japan.

    c. ( )   The Japanese didn't want to buy American products.

19. a. ( )   The U.S. became independent in 1789.

    b. ( )   The new government was established in 1789.

    c. ( )   George Washington became president in 1776.

20. a. ( )   Vanderbilt had only one business, shipping.

    b. ( )   Vanderbilt had only one business, railroads.

    c. ( )   After starting in the shipping business, Vanderbilt went in a new direction.

V. FILL IN

DIRECTIONS: Fill in the blanks with the correct preposition or particle.

Ray Kroc had many jobs before he started his billion dollar business called the McDonald's Corporation. During World War I, he had put in _____ a position as an ambulance driver and got it. After
    1
that, he made a living_____playing piano in nightclubs in
    2
Chicago. Then he worked as a salesman in Florida. His job was to

convince people to invest _____ land in Florida. The next posi-
3

tion he took brought him _____ contact _____ hundreds of
4   5

restaurant owners. He sold a gadget called a Multimixer, which could

mix six milkshakes at the same time. This is how he met the McDonald

brothers. They wanted to buy eight Multimixers for their busy restau-

rant. Mr. Kroc decided to arrange _____ a meeting with them. He
6

was very interested in doing business _____ the McDonald
7

brothers. They met and got _____ to business quickly. The meet-
8

ing paid _____. The McDonalds and Ray Kroc entered _____
9   10

a deal that made history.

Mr. Kroc was sure he could cash _____ _____ the
11   12

need for good, inexpensive food served in a clean and pleasant atmos-

phere. Ten years after he had made a deal _____ the McDonalds,
13

he bought them _____. They signed _____ the business to
14   15

him. Mr. Kroc built _____ the company and helped it branch
16

_____. He even set _____ Hamburger University, where
17   18

the managers were trained.

Ray Kroc had been working over forty years before starting the

McDonald's Corporation. During these years he had to deal _____
19

all types of people. But Ray Kroc was a good businessman, and without

even a high school education, he founded a company that was

valued＿＿＿＿＿＿$4.6 billion by 1980. Now that can probably be
　　　　　20

rounded＿＿＿＿＿＿to $5 billion.
　　　　　　21

VI. PRACTICAL APPLICATION

DIRECTIONS: Read the sentences below about Henry Ford; then rewrite each sentence using the idioms given.

1.   Henry Ford's parents were Irish immigrants who lived on a farm in
     Michigan.
2.   Ford worked in a machinist's shop when he was fifteen years old.
     That is where he learned about machines and engines.
3.   He and some friends formed the Detroit Automobile Company
     which built custom cars for very rich people.
4.   Ford left the company to build racing cars.
5.   In 1903 he and several partners formed the Ford Motor Company.
     They produced the Model T five years later.
6.   Soon the Model T was being produced on an assembly line. The
     company grew and Ford became famous for his assembly-line
     method of production.
7.   Although Ford was against unions, in 1941 he signed a contract with
     the United Auto Workers union.
8.   Gradually, Ford bought stock from other stockholders and gained
     complete control of the Ford Motor Company, which was worth
     billions.

build up	pay off	branch out
buy out	make a living by	do business with
deal with	get down to business	set up
value at	arrange for	make a deal with
sign over		

_____

_____

_____

_____

VII. ADDITIONAL EXERCISES

1. Make up a story about the picture at the beginning of the chapter. Use as many idioms as possible. This exercise can be written or oral.
2. Ask each other questions about the picture. You must use an idiom in your response.
3. Use the lines below the picture for a dictation exercise. The teacher or a student dictates the introductory passage and the students write it.
4. Rewrite the introductory passage in the future tense.

RESIDENCE

Residence

```
334 E. 73 St. only $425
Beaut. 2 BR. sublease. Lux. bldg.
Move-in conditn. Avail. immed.
No fee.
```

INTRODUCTORY PASSAGE

Mr. Barbarino **came across** this advertisement in the Sunday paper. He couldn't **pass up** a two-bedroom apartment for only $425 a month. He, his wife, son, and pets were **cooped up in** a one-bedroom apartment for the same rent. He was really lucky to find that ad.

The next day, Mr. and Mrs. Barbarino went to see the apartment. It was in a luxury building that **towered over** the small brownstones nearby. The entrance, lobby, and elevators **were up to date**.

The apartment itself **looked out on** a quiet side street. The rooms were large and had a lot of closets. But the bathroom was painted shocking pink and the kitchen was **cluttered up** with boxes and suitcases. The tenant promised to **tone down** the walls and **fix** everything **up** before **moving out**.

The Barbarinos liked the apartment very much so they signed the sublease immediately. The tenant asked for two checks—a month's rent and a month's security. He said they could **move in** in one week.

During the week Mr. and Mrs. Barbarino **got rid of** their old furniture and bought antiques to **furnish** their new apartment **with**.

The day of the move, they got a big surprise. The police had **sealed off** 73rd Street. Several other moving trucks were in front of their building. A policeman told Mr. and Mrs. Barbarino that the tenant had been **evicted from** the building; but before he left, he had rented the apartment to ten other families, then disappeared.

NOTES

IDIOMS AND THE POSITION
OF THEIR OBJECTS   *GRAMMATICAL NOTES*   *STYLE*

1. come across   [   ] ————————————————————

——

2. pass [   ]   up _____ informal

_____

3. coop [   ] up in [   ] <u>usually passive</u>   informal

_____

4. tower over [   ] _____

_____

5. be up to   [date] _____

_____

6. look out on   [   ]___<u>object is usually a noun</u>_____

_____

7. clutter [   ] up ___<u>usually passive</u>___ informal

_____

8. tone [   ] down _____

_____

9. fix [   ] up _____ informal

_____

10. move out _____

_____

11. move in _____

_____

12. get rid of [   ] _____ informal

_____

13. furnish [   ] with [   ] often passive
object of the prep. is usually a noun

_____

14. seal [   ] off _____

_____

15. evict [   ] from [   ] usually passive
object of the prep. is usually a noun

_____

Use this page for one or more of the following exercises:

- Write the meaning of the idiom.
- Write sample sentences.
- Look for the idioms in short stories, novels, newspapers, or magazines, and copy the sentences containing them.
- Give examples of appropriate direct objects or objects of the preposition for each idiom that requires an object.
- Practice saying the idioms with correct stress. In general, verbs and particles are stressed, but prepositions are unstressed.

I. DEFINITIONS

DIRECTIONS: Mark the answer that is the closest synonym for the italicized idioms.

1. When I was cleaning out my desk drawer, I *came across* this old picture.

a. (   ) looked for
b. (   ) found
c. (   ) ripped

2. The rent was reasonable and it was in a beautiful neighborhood. We had to *pass* it *up* because we couldn't break our lease.

    a. (   ) not take it
    b. (   ) get more information
    c. (   ) get a lawyer

3. All of us were *cooped up in* that tiny conference room for five hours.

    a. (   ) confined to
    b. (   ) talking in
    c. (   ) having a meeting in

4. The World Trade Center *towers over* the other buildings in lower Manhattan.

    a. (   ) looks like
    b. (   ) blocks
    c. (   ) is much taller than

5. Everything in this kitchen *is up to date.*

    a. (   ) is old
    b. (   ) is used
    c. (   ) is modern

6. His living room *looks out on* a golf course.

    a. (   ) resembles
    b. (   ) is dangerous because of
    c. (   ) faces

7. She collects bric-a-brac and it *clutters up* the whole apartment.

    a. (   ) makes crowded and messy
    b. (   ) makes empty
    c. (   ) makes dirty

8. That paint is too bright. You have to *tone* it *down.*

    a. (   ) make it softer
    b. (   ) return it
    c. (   ) make it brighter

9. Before signing the lease, ask the landlord if he is going to *fix up* the apartment.

    a. ( ) make improvements in
    b. ( ) rent
    c. ( ) increase the rent of

10. He *moved out* when he was old enough to support himself.

    a. ( ) got a job
    b. ( ) traveled a lot
    c. ( ) changed his residence

11. As soon as the present tenant moves out, you can *move in*.

    a. ( ) occupy the apartment
    b. ( ) apply for an apartment
    c. ( ) see the apartment

12. If you *get rid of* these doors, you will have much more room.

    a. ( ) open
    b. ( ) remove
    c. ( ) close

13. They are *furnishing* their apartment *with* French Provincial.

    a. ( ) painting
    b. ( ) decorating
    c. ( ) cleaning

14. While the schoolchildren are playing outside, the police *seal off* the street.

    a. ( ) guard
    b. ( ) leave open
    c. ( ) block

15. He was *evicted from* the building because he didn't pay the rent.

    a. ( ) forced to move out of
    b. ( ) given a job in
    c. ( ) locked up in

II. WORD ASSOCIATION

DIRECTIONS: Two of the three choices below can be used with the idiom. Mark the *two* answers that can be used to complete each sentence correctly.

1. We were surprised when we came across _____.

    a. ( ) your name on the list
    b. ( ) the meeting
    c. ( ) some top-secret documents

2. You can't pass up _____ like that!

    a. ( ) an antique clock
    b. ( ) a broken refrigerator
    c. ( ) a deal

3. Ten prisoners were cooped up in _____ all day.

    a. ( ) this tiny cell
    b. ( ) here
    c. ( ) this huge auditorium

4. That five-story building towers over all the _____ nearby.

    a. ( ) houses
    b. ( ) skyscrapers
    c. ( ) cottages

5. That _____ is certainly up to date.

    a. ( ) station wagon
    b. ( ) outfit
    c. ( ) horse

6. The living room looks out on _____.

    a. ( ) a view
    b. ( ) a brick wall
    c. ( ) the garden

7. The _____ cluttered up the room.

       a. ( ) doll
       b. ( ) bric-a-brac
       c. ( ) garbage

8. You should tone down _____.

       a. ( ) the color of the walls
       b. ( ) the paint
       c. ( ) that light blue paint

9. He has to finish fixing up _____ before his mother-in-law arrives.

       a. ( ) the house
       b. ( ) the guest room
       c. ( ) the television

10. The _____ wants to move out.

       a. ( ) writer
       b. ( ) neighborhood
       c. ( ) senior citizen

11. The _____ is moving in today.

       a. ( ) truck
       b. ( ) couple
       c. ( ) new tenant

12. The first thing she wants to do is get rid of _____.

       a. ( ) those ugly venetian blinds
       b. ( ) those old-fashioned sinks
       c. ( ) the roof

13. The hotel room was furnished with _____.

       a. ( ) modern furniture
       b. ( ) beautiful antiques
       c. ( ) two closets

14. The manager decided to seal off the _____.

       a. ( ) exit
       b. ( ) water
       c. ( ) passage

15. The tenant was evicted from _____.

       a. ( ) the building
       b. ( ) the apartment house
       c. ( ) the city

III. THE POSITION OF THE OBJECT

DIRECTIONS: Fill in *one* of the blanks (a or b) in each sentence with the object given in parentheses. *Two* of the sentences do not have objects. For those sentences, do not write anything.

1. They sealed _____ off _____. (it)
                     a   b

2. We came _____ across _____. (it)
                  a   b

3. The building is up_____ to _____. (date)
                          a   b

4. Don't pass _____ up _____. (it)
                     a   b

5. That skyscraper towers _____ over _____. (the
                                 a   b

   others)

6. You need to fix _____ up _____. (it)
                         a   b

7. The tenant was evicted _____ from _____. (the
                                 a   b

   building)

8. He is going to get rid_____ of _____. (it)
                              a   b

9. We will tone _____ down _____. (it)
                      a   b

10. In two weeks we will move_____ in _____. (it)
                                  a   b

11. The apartment was furnished _____ with _____ .
                                        a   b

(modern furniture)

12. They don't want to move _____ out _____ . (it)
                                       a   b

13. He cluttered _____ up _____ . (it)
                          a   b

14. They cooped _____ up _____ in a tiny office.   (us)
                         a   b

15. It doesn't look out _____ on _____ . (the park)
                                  a   b

IV. LISTENING COMPREHENSION ANSWER SHEET

DIRECTIONS: You will hear a situation presented in one or two sentences. Listen to each statement and mark the response that most closely corresponds to the situation.

1. a. ( ) The rent was too high.
    b. ( ) There was too much work to be done.
    c. ( ) The necessary repairs would be too expensive.

2. a. ( ) She put up venetian blinds because she doesn't like the sun.
    b. ( ) She removed the blinds because she likes sunlight.
    c. ( ) She is blind.

3. a. ( ) They will move in on Tuesday.
    b. ( ) They will move in right away.
    c. ( ) They will move in on Sunday.

4. a. ( ) Mark's windows face Park Avenue.
    b. ( ) Mark's windows face 79th Street.
    c. ( ) Mark enters his building on 79th Street.

5. a. ( ) The bathroom is crowded with Debbie's dirty laundry.

   b. ( ) Lois and Debbie always fight in the bathroom.

   c. ( ) Lois always leaves her dirty laundry all over the bathroom.

6. a. ( ) The bathroom is in excellent condition.

   b. ( ) In general, the apartment is a good deal.

   c. ( ) They are not going to take the apartment because it is not a good deal.

7. a. ( ) Originally there were two exits, but one was closed.

   b. ( ) Three exits were enough.

   c. ( ) One exit had been closed and only two were open.

8. a. ( ) The apartment walls are too pale.

   b. ( ) They probably don't like such intense color on the walls.

   c. ( ) They don't want the apartment anyway.

9. a. ( ) They were evicted from the apartment.

   b. ( ) The apartment is vacant.

   c. ( ) The tenant is still there.

10. a. ( ) The secretaries want better working conditions.

    b. ( ) The secretaries don't like their boss.

    c. ( ) The secretaries can't open the window all day.

11. a. ( ) The billboards surprised me.

    b. ( ) I was looking for the billboards.

    c. ( ) I couldn't find the billboards.

12. a. ( ) The Empire State Building is taller.

    b. ( ) The World Trade Center is taller.

    c. ( ) The two buildings are close to each other.

13. a. ( ) The dentist works faster now because of his new equipment.

 b. ( ) The dentist likes expensive furniture.

 c. ( ) The patients must pay more money because the dentist bought new equipment.

14. a. ( ) That department store really has the newest items.

 b. ( ) Customers usually want the latest merchandise.

 c. ( ) Their business is very good.

15. a. ( ) The person wants to leave the apartment before the end of the lease.

 b. ( ) The person wants to leave the apartment when the lease is finished.

 c. ( ) The person lost his deposit because he moved out.

V. FILL IN

DIRECTIONS: Fill in the blanks with the correct preposition or particle.

UNFURNISHED APARTMENTS—Three, Four, or Five Rooms

Are you cooped_____ in a small apartment? Don't pass this
                              1

_____! You won't come_____anything like this
              2   3

again. The Graystone towers_____all the buildings nearby.
                                            4

All apartments look_____on either the river or a park.
                            5

All equipment is_____ to date. No need to fix anything
                        6

_____. Move_____ right away. Furnish it_____
        7   8   9

whatever you have; it will look great. You will never want to

move_____. This building is so safe you will get rid
            10

_____ your worries about the big city.
        11

Call 859-9327 today!

VI. PRACTICAL APPLICATION

DIRECTIONS: Use the information below in a letter to a friend in the United States about your new apartment. Try to use as many idioms as possible. Refer to the list on pages 38, 39, and 40 if necessary.

Old Apartment

1. one small room, no windows
2. crowded with books and clothes
3. old-fashioned building
4. used furniture
5. faced a fire house
6. no room for my desk
7. balcony was blocked

New Apartment

1. found a sign outside the building
2. previous tenant was expelled
3. in a tall building
4. needs to be painted
5. walls are purple and aqua
6. cheap rent; good deal
7. occupied the apartment on Monday

Dear _____,

_____

_____

_____

_____

_____

_____

_____

_____

_____

Sincerely yours,

_____

VII. ADDITIONAL EXERCISES

1. Make up a story about the picture at the beginning of the chapter. Use as many idioms as possible. This exercise can be written or oral.
2. Ask each other questions about the picture. You must use an idiom in your response.
3. Use the lines below the picture for a dictation exercise. The teacher or a student dictates the introductory passage and the students write it.
4. Change each sentence in the introductory passage to a question.

CRIME

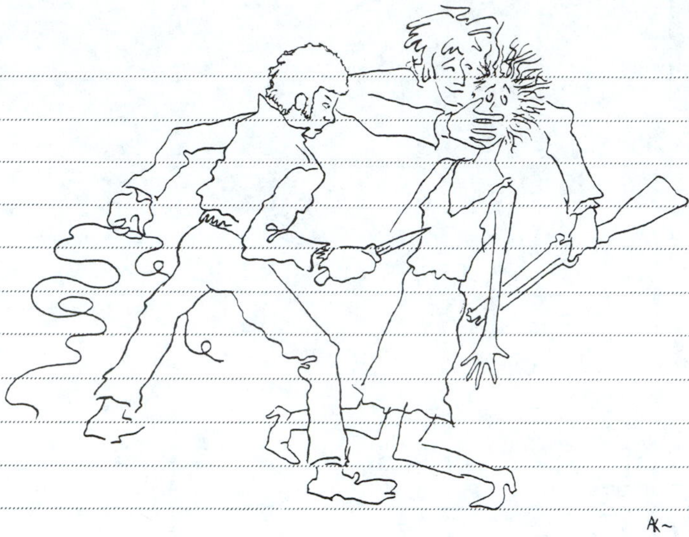

Crime

INTRODUCTORY PASSAGE

In Cold Blood*

It was Friday, November 13, 1959. Mr. Clutter signed a $40,000 life insurance policy. The next day he was killed. His wife and two children didn't collect the insurance. They were all **gunned down** the same day.

It happened in a small town in Kansas. Two ex-cons, Dick and Perry, expected to find a lot of money in a safe in the Clutter house. Dick's friend from jail had told him that Mr. Clutter was very rich. The robbers **broke in, prowled around, tied up** the whole family, and killed each one in cold blood. Dick and Perry **made off with** about $40.

They went to Mexico, came back to the United States, traveled from state to state, but all that time Perry didn't believe they would **get away with** it. He was right. They were **picked up** in Las Vegas and **locked up.** It was a hard job for the detectives. They had only one clue, a footprint in blood; and one witness, Dick's old friend from jail.

When the case was **brought to trial** Dick wouldn't **own up to** the killings. He said he hadn't killed anyone and **put the blame on** Perry. Perry **confessed to** killing Mr. Clutter and his son, but **accused** Dick **of** shooting Mrs. Clutter and her daughter. Both men were **charged with** murder and both were **convicted of** murder in the first degree. The judge **sentenced** them to death.

For five more years they **were behind bars** before they **paid for** their crime. All that time Dick and Perry hoped to **escape from** jail but there is only one way out of Death Row. They were hanged on April 14, 1965.

*Based on the novel, *In Cold Blood*, by Truman Capote.

NOTES

	IDIOMS AND THE POSITION OF THEIR OBJECTS	GRAMMATICAL NOTES	STYLE
1.	gun [ ] down		informal
2.	break in		
3.	prowl around [ ]	object is not necessary	
4.	tie [ ] up		
5.	make off with [ ]		
6.	get away with [ ]		informal
7.	pick [ ] up	often passive	
8.	lock [ ] up	usually passive	
9.	bring [ ] to [trial]	usually passive	legal

10. own up to   [   ]   _____

_____

11. put   [the blame]   on   [   ]   _____

_____

12. confess to   [   ]   _____

_____

13. accuse   [   ]   of   [   ]   often passive; often followed by *-ing* form

_____

14. charge   [   ]   with   [   ]   usually passive   legal

_____

15. convict   [   ]   of   [   ]   usually passive   legal

_____

16. sentence   [   ]   to   [   ]   usually passive / object of the prep.   legal / is usually a noun

_____

17. be behind   [bars]   _____

_____

18. pay for   [   ]   _____

_____

19. escape from   [   ]   _____

_____

Use this page for one or more of the following exercises:

- Write the meaning of the idiom.
- Write sample sentences.
- Look for the idioms in short stories, novels, newspapers, or magazines, and copy the sentences containing them.
- Give examples of appropriate direct objects or objects of the preposition for each idiom that requires an object.
- Practice saying the idioms with correct stress. In general, verbs and particles are stressed, but prepositions are unstressed.

I. DEFINITIONS

DIRECTIONS: Mark the answer that is the closest synonym for the italicized idioms.

1. They were all *gunned down* the same day.

   a. ( ) putting down their guns
   b. ( ) shot unmercifully
   c. ( ) beaten with guns

2. The robbers *broke in.*

   a. ( ) needed money
   b. ( ) got hurt
   c. ( ) forced their way in

3. The robbers *prowled around.*

   a. ( ) walked carefully and quietly
   b. ( ) killed everybody
   c. ( ) screamed

4. The robbers *tied up* the whole family.

   a. ( ) put ties on
   b. ( ) bound with string or rope
   c. ( ) attempted to kill

5.   Dick and Perry *made off with* about $40.

        a.   ( )   earned
        b.   ( )   printed
        c.   ( )   stole and left quickly with

6.   Perry didn't believe they would *get away with* it.

        a.   ( )   not be punished for
        b.   ( )   have a plan for
        c.   ( )   take a vacation with

7.   They were *picked up* in Las Vegas.

        a.   ( )   lost
        b.   ( )   found and arrested
        c.   ( )   given a trial

8.   They were *locked up* in Las Vegas.

        a.   ( )   imprisoned
        b.   ( )   sent to the courtroom
        c.   ( )   forced to go home

9.   The case was *brought to trial.*

        a.   ( )   tried in a court of law
        b.   ( )   dismissed
        c.   ( )   talked about

10. Dick wouldn't *own up to* the killings.

        a.   ( )   commit
        b.   ( )   talk about
        c.   ( )   admit responsibility for

11. He *put the blame on* Perry.

        a.   ( )   forgave
        b.   ( )   accused
        c.   ( )   attacked

12.   Perry *confessed to* killing Mr. Clutter.

a. ( ) confused
b. ( ) enjoyed
c. ( ) admitted

13.   Perry *accused* Dick *of* shooting Mrs. Clutter.

a. ( ) said Dick was guilty of
b. ( ) arrested for
c. ( ) admitted to

14.   Both men were *charged with* murder.

a. ( ) accused of
b. ( ) proven to be guilty of
c. ( ) asked to commit

15.   Both were *convicted of* murder in the first degree.

a. ( ) found guilty of
b. ( ) thought to be guilty of
c. ( ) tried for

16.   The judge *sentenced* them *to* death.

a. ( ) stated the punishment
b. ( ) gave a speech about
c. ( ) suggested the punishment of

17.   For five more years they *were behind bars.*

a. ( ) were in court
b. ( ) were free
c. ( ) were in jail

18.   They *paid for* their crime.

a. ( ) were punished for
b. ( ) collected money for
c. ( ) paid their lawyers for

19.   Dick and Perry hoped to *escape from* jail.

        a.   ( )   be released from
        b.   ( )   remain in
        c.   ( )   break out of

II. WORD ASSOCIATION

DIRECTIONS: Two of the three choices below can be used with the idiom. Mark the *two* answers that can be used to complete each sentence correctly.

1.   She owned up to _____.

        a.   ( )   the confession
        b.   ( )   stealing the gems
        c.   ( )   giving the top-secret document
                  to the journalist

2.   He paid for _____.

        a.   ( )   his blunder
        b.   ( )   his punishment
        c.   ( )   his crime

3.   _____ was brought to trial.

        a.   ( )   The case
        b.   ( )   The defendant
        c.   ( )   The witness

4.   He was convicted of _____.

        a.   ( )   premeditated murder
        b.   ( )   armed robbery
        c.   ( )   the case

5. The rebel gunned down _____.

    a. ( )   the ambassador
    b. ( )   the weapons
    c. ( )   the bystanders

6. They escaped from _____.

    a. ( )   captivity
    b. ( )   a maximum security prison
    c. ( )   fear

7. _____ is behind bars now.

    a. ( )   The killer
    b. ( )   The gangster
    c. ( )   The murder case

8. He got away with _____.

    a. ( )   the cover-up
    b. ( )   his good behavior
    c. ( )   his obnoxious behavior

9. The guest made off with _____.

    a. ( )   the cash
    b. ( )   the painting
    c. ( )   the robbery

10. _____ broke in.

    a. ( )   A German shepherd
    b. ( )   A street gang
    c. ( )   A burglar

11. The convict was sentenced to _____.

    a. ( )   life imprisonment
    b. ( )   murder
    c. ( )   the electric chair

12. _____ was prowling around.

    a. ( ) The victim
    b. ( ) The thief
    c. ( ) The armed bandit

13. He was charged with _____.

    a. ( ) possession of heroin
    b. ( ) drunken driving
    c. ( ) being a lady-killer

14. They tied up _____.

    a. ( ) the package
    b. ( ) the building
    c. ( ) the guard

15. The police picked up _____.

    a. ( ) the escaped convict
    b. ( ) the killer's look-alike
    c. ( ) the robbery

16. She confessed to _____.

    a. ( ) stealing the money
    b. ( ) the disgraceful crime
    c. ( ) not committing the murder

17. _____ was locked up.

    a. ( ) The wrong man
    b. ( ) The war criminal
    c. ( ) The door

18. The victim's family put the blame on _____.

    a. ( ) the police
    b. ( ) the icy roads
    c. ( ) the youngster's future

19.   He was accused of _____.

      a.   ( )   starting the fire
      b.   ( )   perjury
      c.   ( )   the police

III. THE POSITION OF THE OBJECT

DIRECTIONS: Fill in *one* of the blanks (a or b) in each sentence with the object given in parentheses. *One* of the sentences has no object. For that sentence, do not write anything.

1.   Nobody has ever escaped _____ from _____.   (it)
                                       a   b

2.   The burglars tied _____ up _____.   (us)
                      a   b

3.   The lunatic gunned _____ down _____.   (her)
                        a   b

4.   They brought _____ to _____ trial quickly.   (it)
                  a   b

5.   She made off _____ with _____.   (it)
                a   b

6.   You won't get away _____ with _____.   (it)
                  a   b

7.   Lock _____ up _____!   (them)
        a   b

8.   The police picked _____ up _____.   (him)
                a   b

9.   He has been convicted _____ of _____.   (it)
                  a   b

10.   She wasn't accused _____ of _____.   (that)
                  a   b

11.   They prowled _____ around _____.   (the house)
                a   b

12.   He paid _____ for _____.   (it)
              a   b

13.   They were both charged _____ with _____.
                        a   b

     (murder)

14.   He didn't want to own up _____ to _____.   (it)
                          a   b

15. They were sentenced _____ a to _____ b . (death)

16. He has already confessed _____ a to _____ b . (it)

17. Don't put the blame _____ a on _____ b . (him)

18. The killer is already _____ a behind _____ b . (bars)

19. He broke _____ a in _____ b during the weekend. (it)

IV. LISTENING COMPREHENSION ANSWER SHEET

DIRECTIONS: You will hear a situation presented in one or two sentences. Listen to each statement and mark the response that most closely corresponds to the situation.

1. a. ( ) The robber spent seven years in prison.
   b. ( ) The robber was sent to prison for twenty-two months.
   c. ( ) The robber was arrested in a bar.
   d. ( ) The robber was in prison less than two years.

2. a. ( ) He entered his victims' apartments by breaking the locks.
   b. ( ) He was put in jail for murder.
   c. ( ) He locked the doors of the women's apartments.
   d. ( ) He was put in jail for sixty-three years.

3. a. ( ) He was punished for murder.
   b. ( ) He was never punished because he was so cute.
   c. ( ) The cute little boy committed murder.
   d. ( ) He had a way of murdering boys.

4. a. ( ) Raskolnikov's sister escapes with the jewelry.
   b. ( ) Raskolnikov didn't get any jewelry.
   c. ( ) After the murders, Raskolnikov escapes with some jewelry.
   d. ( ) The only crime in the novel is robbery.

5. a. ( ) She got out of jail the first day she was behind bars.

    b. ( ) It didn't bother her to be in jail.

    c. ( ) She didn't want to stay in jail.

    d. ( ) She was never arrested.

6. a. ( ) His parents said it was the school's fault.

    b. ( ) The school said it was the boy's parents' fault.

    c. ( ) His parents blamed themselves.

    d. ( ) His parents committed suicide.

7. a. ( ) She was afraid a burglar was inside her apartment.

    b. ( ) She saw a body in her apartment.

    c. ( ) She was afraid of the dark.

    d. ( ) She looked all over the apartment.

8. a. ( ) If a person steals something, his hand is cut off in Islamic countries.

    b. ( ) In Muslim countries a thief must pay back what he steals. There is no additional punishment.

    c. ( ) Stealing is not considered a crime in Muslim countries.

    d. ( ) In Muslim countries the punishment for any crime is amputation of the hand.

9. a. ( ) The newspaper report said that the policeman was murdered.

    b. ( ) The policeman admitted that he murdered somebody.

    c. ( ) The policeman said it was his duty to kill.

    d. ( ) The report said the policeman killed somebody while he wasn't working. It hasn't been proven yet.

10. a. ( ) The detectives always made the same knot.

    b. ( ) Before the victims were killed, they were tied up.

    c. ( ) The killer did not tie up his victims.

    d. ( ) The detectives found the killer when he was making a knot.

11. a. ( ) Son of Sam killed somebody because of a parking ticket.

    b. ( ) The police discovered who murdered Son of Sam.

    c. ( ) Son of Sam was caught before he got a parking ticket.

    d. ( ) Son of Sam was caught after he got a parking ticket.

12. a. ( ) The boy said it was the first time he stole something.

    b. ( ) The teenager admitted stealing thirty records previously.

    c. ( ) The store detective didn't see the boy stealing the record.

    d. ( ) The store detective caught the boy with thirty records.

13. a. ( ) He left his position as Vice-President and went to jail.

    b. ( ) He went to jail for three years.

    c. ( ) He should have added $10,000 to his income tax report.

    d. ( ) It was said that the former Vice-President didn't report $29,500 on his income tax report.

14. a. ( ) The eyewitness heard about the shooting.

    b. ( ) He probably thought it was better to admit his crime because somebody had seen the shooting.

    c. ( ) There weren't any witnesses.

    d. ( ) He shot the witness as soon as possible.

15. a. ( ) The burglars went to the Democratic Party's head-quarters to steal something.

    b. ( ) The burglars were never caught.

    c. ( ) They entered the building legally.

    d. ( ) The burglars worked at the Democratic Party's head-quarters.

V. FILL IN

DIRECTIONS: Fill in the blanks with the correct preposition or particle.

It was Friday, November 13, 1959. Mr. Clutter signed a $40,000 life insurance policy. The next day he was killed. His wife and two children didn't collect the insurance. They were all gunned _____ the same day.
                                                                      1

It happened in a small town in Kansas. Two ex-cons, Dick and Perry, expected to find a lot of money in a safe in the Clutter house. Dick's friend from jail had told him that Mr. Clutter was very rich. The robbers broke _____, prowled _____, tied _____ the
                    2   3   4
whole family, and killed each one in cold blood. Dick and Perry made _____ with about $40.
              5

They went to Mexico, came back to the United States, traveled from state to state, but all that time Perry didn't believe they would get _____ with it. He was right. They were picked _____ in Las
           6   7
Vegas and locked _____. It was a hard job for the detectives. They
                       8
had only one clue, a footprint in blood; and one witness, Dick's old friend from jail.

When the case was brought _____ trial Dick wouldn't own
                                 9
_____ to the killings. He said he hadn't killed anyone and put
       10
the blame _____ Perry. Perry confessed _____ killing Mr.
              11   12

Clutter and his son, but accused Dick _____13_____ shooting Mrs.

Clutter and her daughter. Both men were charged _____14_____ murder

and both were convicted _____15_____ murder in the first degree. The

judge sentenced them _____16_____ death.

For five more years they were _____17_____ bars before they

paid _____18_____ their crime. All that time Dick and Perry hoped to

escape _____19_____ jail but there is only one way out of Death Row.

They were hanged on April 14, 1965.

VI. PRACTICAL APPLICATION

DIRECTIONS: The following paragraphs are about crimes. Find a sentence with an idiom about crime and write the idiom in the parentheses. Then rewrite the sentence in your own words *without* using the idiom.

1.   The father said his five children were there when the gunmen broke in. The youngest was his newborn baby.
2.   His followers were accused of fixing the elections to ensure an overwhelming victory. After months of rioting, he agreed to void the election.
3.   Two teenagers have been charged with starting 13 fires. The police describe it as a wave of arson that has ruined over a hundred houses in this area.
4.   The police said it seemed that the robbers had made off with over $40 million in securities as well as a large amount of cash.
5.   Philip Stevens was convicted of killing his pregnant wife and three young children. Mr. Stevens, an emergency room surgeon, killed the four members of his family then inflicted wounds on himself to conceal his role in the crime.

1. (   ) _____

_____

_____

2. (   ) _____

_____

_____

3. (   ) _____

_____

_____

4. (   ) _____

_____

_____

5. (   ) _____

_____

_____

VII. ADDITIONAL EXERCISES

1. Make up a story about the picture at the beginning of the chapter. Use as many idioms as possible. This exercise can be written or oral.
2. Ask each other questions about the picture. You must use an idiom in your response.
3. Use the lines below the picture for a dictation exercise. The teacher or a student dictates the introductory passage and the students write it.
4. Rewrite the introductory passage in the present tense.

5

LOVE

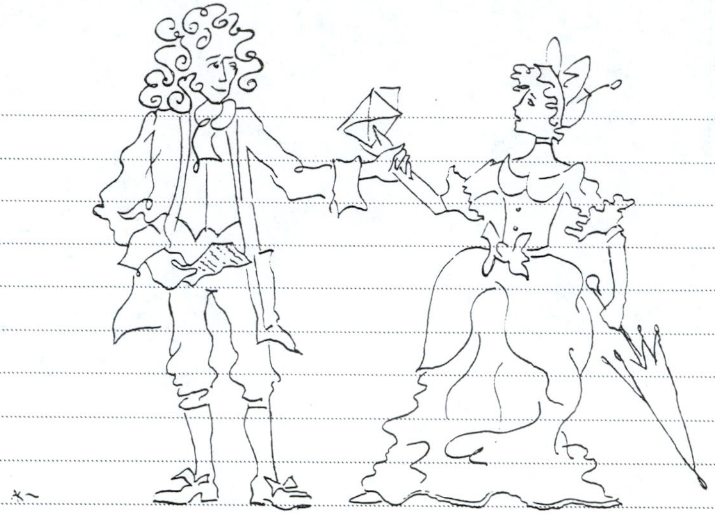

Love

INTRODUCTORY PASSAGE

Dear Mother and Father,

My mistress died recently. On her deathbed she asked her son, Mr. B, to **look after** me. But the problem is that he **can't take his eyes off** me. In fact, he **flirts with** me all the time. The other servants say he **has a crush on** me. What do you think I should do?

Your loving daughter,
Pamela Andrews

Dear Pamela,

We are terribly afraid that Mr. B **has designs on** you. Don't forget you are only fifteen years old and your master can **wind you around his little finger.**

Your worried parents

Dearest Mother and Father,

Thank goodness I **get along with** the housekeeper, Mrs. Jervis. It is wonderful that I can **confide in** her. She says I have **swept** Mr. B **off his feet,** and that he **is infatuated with** me. I still don't believe he will try to **have an affair with** me! If he **makes a pass at** me I will do whatever I can to come home to you.

Your devoted daughter,
Pamela

My Dear Parents,

I am like a prisoner now. Mr. B thinks we should **live together** and if we are happy, he will **propose to** me in one year. He has already tried to **make love with** me! I fainted. When I could speak again, I begged him to let me go home.

Pamela Andrews

Dear Parents,

Mr. B became so angry that he **threw** me **out.** On the way to your house, I received a letter from him. He wrote that he was very sick and wanted me to return. I went back immediately. I guess I had **fallen in love with** him.

When we **got together,** Mr. B felt much better and I did too. I am happy to tell you that we just got married.

Now I can sign my letter,

Pamela B

Pamela was written in 1739 by Samuel Richardson, a London printer. He began by writing a book of model letters but finished by writing a novel. In fact, *Pamela* is considered the first modern novel.

NOTES

IDIOMS AND THE POSITION
OF THEIR OBJECTS   *GRAMMATICAL NOTES*   *STYLE*

1. look after   [   ]   _____

_____

2. (can't) take   [one's eyes]   off   [   ]   _____

_____

3. flirt with   [   ]   _____

_____

4. have   [a crush]   on   [   ]   _____ informal

_____

5. have   [designs]   on   [   ]_____ informal

_____

6. wind   [   ]   around   [one's little finger]   _____ informal

_____

7. get along with   [   ]   _____

_____

8. confide in   [   ]   _____

_____

9. sweep   [   ]   off   [his/her feet]   _____ informal

_____

10. be infatuated with   [   ]   _____

_____

11. have   [an affair]   with   [   ]   _____

_____

12. make   [a pass]   at   [   ]   _____ informal

_____

13. live together _____

_____

14. propose to [   ] _____

_____

15. make [love] with [   ] _____

_____

16. throw [   ] out _____ informal

_____

17. fall in [love] with [   ] _____

_____

18. get together _____

_____

Use this page for one or more of the following exercises:

- Write the meaning of the idiom.
- Write sample sentences.
- Look for the idioms in short stories, novels, newspapers, or magazines, and copy the sentences containing them.
- Give examples of appropriate direct objects or objects of the preposition for each idiom that requires an object.
- Practice saying the idioms with correct stress. In general, verbs and particles are stressed, but prepositions are unstressed.

I. DEFINITIONS

DIRECTIONS: Match each idiom on the left with its correct definition on the right. Write the letter of the definition on the line next to the idiom.

1. look after __
2. can't take one's eyes off __
3. flirt with __
4. have a crush on __
5. have designs on __
6. wind around one's little finger __
7. get along with __
8. confide in __
9. sweep off his/her feet __
10. be infatuated with __
11. have an affair with __
12. make a pass at __
13. live together __
14. propose to __
15. make love with __
16. throw out __
17. fall in love with __
18. get together __

a. manipulate somebody through charm
b. tell somebody something in confidence
c. make somebody fall in love with you
d. love foolishly
e. meet, see a person
f. ask somebody to marry you
g. take responsibility for
h. be very interested in somebody
i. date and have relations with somebody you are not married to
j. suggest sexual attraction by a word or gesture
k. live in the same house even if not married
l. plan to have intimate relations with somebody
m. have a good relationship
n. have sexual relations
o. begin to love somebody
p. expel somebody
q. stare at somebody because of interest in that person
r. do something to show an interest in another person

II. WORD ASSOCIATION

DIRECTIONS: Two of the three choices below can be used with the idiom. Mark the *two* answers that can be used to complete each sentence correctly.

1. Helen confided in _____.

   a. ( ) her best friend
   b. ( ) her diary
   c. ( ) psychology

2. We got together for _____.

        a. ( ) a drink
        b. ( ) happiness
        c. ( ) brunch

3. She gets along with _____.

        a. ( ) her job
        b. ( ) her colleagues
        c. ( ) her husband

4. She fell in love with _____.

        a. ( ) her teacher
        b. ( ) a boy who doesn't speak her language
        c. ( ) humanity

5. Jimmy has a crush on _____.

        a. ( ) a girl in his class
        b. ( ) his poodle
        c. ( ) his tutor

6. _____ will live together in San Francisco.

        a. ( ) Karen and her fiancé
        b. ( ) The couple
        c. ( ) The teenager

7. He flirted with _____.

        a. ( ) a box of chocolates
        b. ( ) the salesgirl
        c. ( ) the stranger at the next table

8. She had an affair with _____.

        a. ( ) her husband
        b. ( ) her husband's best friend
        c. ( ) her boss

9. Janice must look after _____.

        a. ( ) her younger sister
        b. ( ) her great grandmother
        c. ( ) her lost puppy

10. Michael has designs on _____.

        a. ( ) the highest position
        b. ( ) his new assistant
        c. ( ) his blind date

11. _____ couldn't take his eyes off the saleswoman.

        a. ( ) The customer
        b. ( ) The kitten
        c. ( ) The buyer

12. It seems that she can wind _____ around her little finger.

        a. ( ) her ring
        b. ( ) her parents
        c. ( ) her counselor

13. He swept _____ off her feet.

        a. ( ) his date
        b. ( ) his six-day-old daughter
        c. ( ) the actress

14. She is infatuated with _____.

        a. ( ) the new man in her life
        b. ( ) her job
        c. ( ) her latest husband

15. Thomas made a pass at _____.

        a. ( ) a woman on the bus
        b. ( ) her pretty face
        c. ( ) the waitress

16. John is going to propose to _____.

          a. (   ) a girl he met last week
          b. (   ) his boss, Mr. Richmond
          c. (   ) his high school sweetheart

17. He made love with _____ in the motel.

          a. (   ) his wife
          b. (   ) his car
          c. (   ) his girlfriend

18. She threw _____ out.

          a. (   ) her husband
          b. (   ) the angry customer
          c. (   ) herself

III. THE POSITION OF THE OBJECT

DIRECTIONS: Fill in *one* of the blanks (a or b) in each sentence with the object given in parentheses. *Two* of the sentences do not have objects. For those sentences, do not write anything.

1. He threw _____ out _____. (her)
          a   b

2. He flirts _____ with _____. (them)
          a   b

3. You can confide _____ in _____. (him)
                    a   b

4. She looked _____ after _____. (him)
              a   b

5. They don't want to get married but they will live_____
                                                    a

    together _____. (it)
            b

6. He has designs _____ on _____. (her)
                  a   b

7. She doesn't get along _____ with _____. (him)
                        a   b

8. He swept _____ off _____ her feet.   (her)
        a   b

9. She is infatuated _____ with _____.   (him)
                       a   b

10. Now we can get _____ together _____ more
                   a   b

    often.   (it)

11. She fell in love _____ with _____.   (him)
                     a   b

12. He proposed _____ to _____.   (her)
                a   b

13. He made love _____ with _____.   (her)
                 a   b

14. She couldn't take her eyes _____ off _____.   (him)
                               a   b

15. She has a crush _____ on _____.   (him)
                    a   b

16. He can wind _____ around _____ his little finger.
                a   b

    (her)

17. She is having an affair _____ with _____.   (him)
                           a   b

18. He made a pass _____ at _____.   (her)
                   a   b

IV. LISTENING COMPREHENSION ANSWER SHEET

Part I

DIRECTIONS: You will hear a situation followed by a question. After you hear each question, read the three choices and mark the response that answers the question correctly.

1. a. ( )   He captivated her.

    b. ( )   He was attracted to her.

    c. ( )   He couldn't look at her.

2. a. ( )   Humbert planned to make love with Lolita.

   b. ( )   Humbert was drawing pictures of Lolita.

   c. ( )   Lolita discovered Humbert's diary.

3. a. ( )   He took responsibility for her.

   b. ( )   He killed Lolita.

   c. ( )   He died.

4. a. ( )   Yes, but they lived in hotels instead of an apartment.

   b. ( )   No, but they traveled together and shared hotel rooms.

   c. ( )   Yes, they got married in a hotel.

5. a. ( )   Humbert becomes her husband.

   b. ( )   They meet once again.

   c. ( )   Lolita escapes.

Part II

DIRECTIONS: You will hear a short dialogue followed by a question. After you hear each question, read the three choices and mark the response that answers the question correctly.

1. a. ( )   When they began to get along.

   b. ( )   When they decided to get married.

   c. ( )   When he cancelled a date.

2. a. ( )   He passed Margaret in the corridor.

   b. ( )   He winked or smiled to show that he was interested in her.

   c. ( )   He saw that she was interested in him.

3. a. ( )   She met a terrible man.

   b. ( )   She was infatuated with him.

   c. ( )   She was crushed by what happened at the party.

4. a. ( )   It was quite peaceful.

   b. ( )   They were busy all the time with the Italian men.

   c. ( )   It wasn't very good.

5. a. ( )   She has tiny fingers.

    b. ( )   She falls in love with a lot of guys.

    c. ( )   She is manipulative.

V. FILL IN

DIRECTIONS: Fill in the blanks with an idiom about love. The meaning of the idiom is given below each line. Edit your work to be sure your answers are grammatically correct.

Darling Susan,

When I met you at the party the other night I _____
_____ 1 (began to

_____ you. You looked so beautiful in your silk dress, I just
love)

couldn't _____ you. When I saw John _____
2 (stop staring at)   3(suggesting

_____ you I was terribly jealous.
sexual attraction)

As I explained, Martha and I have been _____
4(sharing the same

_____ for two years but we are very different, and we don't
house)

_____ each other at all. I'm not a playboy
5 (have a good relationship with)

and I don't like to _____ other women, but you're
6 (show an interest in)

not just another woman. You're very special. Please don't think I just want

to _____ you. I love you! I want to _____
7(have relations with)   8 (meet/see)

with you as soon as possible and spend as much time as I can with

you.

Maybe it looks like I _____ you, but I think
9 (am foolishly in love with)

it is real love. You have _____
10 (made me fall in love with you).

Love and kisses,
Michael

VI. ADDITIONAL EXERCISES

1. Make up a story about the picture at the beginning of the chapter. Use as many idioms as possible. This exercise can be written or oral.
2. Ask each other questions about the picture. You must use an idiom in your response.
3. Use the lines below the picture for a dictation exercise. The teacher or a student dictates the introductory passage and the students write it.
4. Rewrite the introductory passage as a story. Do not use the letter format.

6

FASHION

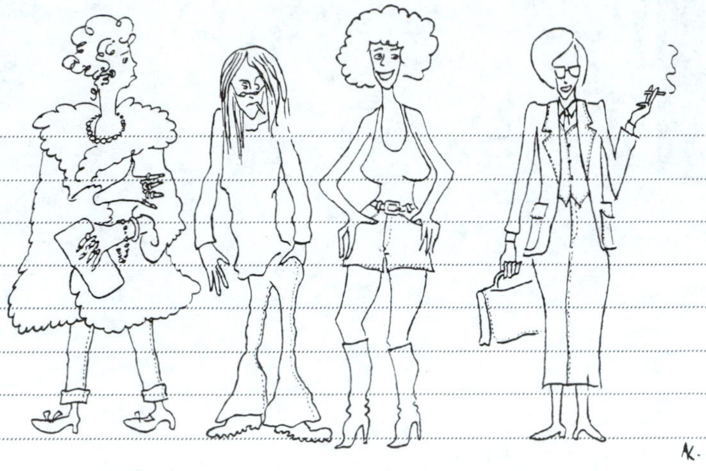

Fashion

INTRODUCTORY PASSAGE

It happened during the California Gold Rush. An American sailmaker moved to the West Coast with a large supply of blue canvas and orange thread. His name was Levi Strauss.

Strauss had a problem in California. Nobody wanted to buy his supplies; everybody was too busy digging for gold. "Gold diggers don't need sails," he thought, "they need strong trousers." So Strauss **came up with** a clever idea—to **make** trousers for the gold diggers **out of** his material.

He hired a saddlemaker and they **put together** the blue canvas, the orange thread, and copper rivets to produce the strongest trousers ever made. In 1850, the first blue jeans **came out.**

Once they **came in,** Levi's never **went out of fashion.** Workmen **put** them **on;** children **pull** them **on** and **roll** them **up;** cowboys never **take** them **off;** even presidents **show up in** them.

Americans, in general, don't like to **dress up.** They prefer to **wear** a pair of jeans which they can **zip up** in a second. Jeans **go with** everything—a sweatshirt or a mink coat. People who **keep up with the times** buy designer jeans. All over the world jeans **are in vogue.**

Levi Strauss didn't need to dig for gold; his invention was a gold mine.

NOTES

IDIOMS AND THE POSITION OF THEIR OBJECTS		*GRAMMATICAL NOTES*	*STYLE*
1. come up with	[ ]	_____	informal

2. make   [   ]   out of   [   ] <u>object of the prep. is usually a noun</u>

3. put   [   ]   together _____

4. come out _____

5. come in _____

6. go out of   [fashion] _____

7. put   [   ]   on _____

8. pull   [   ]   on _____ *informal*

9. roll   [   ]   up _____

10. take   [   ]   off _____

11. show up in   [   ] _____

12. dress up _____

_____

13. zip [   ] up _____ informal

_____

14. go with [   ] _____

_____

15. keep up with   [the times] _____

_____

16. be in   [vogue] _____

_____

Use this page for one or more of the following exercises:

- Write the meaning of the idiom.
- Write sample sentences.
- Look for the idioms in short stories, novels, newspapers, or magazines, and copy the sentences containing them.
- Give examples of appropriate direct objects or objects of the preposition for each idiom that requires an object.
- Practice saying the idioms with correct stress. In general, verbs and particles are stressed, but prepositions are unstressed.

I. DEFINITIONS

DIRECTIONS: Mark the answer that is the closest synonym for the italicized idioms.

1. The young salesman *came up with* a money-saving idea.

    a. ( ) bought
    b. ( ) exchanged
    c. ( ) found

2. The bedspread was *made out of* tiny pieces of material.

    a. ( )   produced from
    b. ( )   ripped into
    c. ( )   covered with

3. The jeweler *put* the watch *together* again.

    a. ( )   assembled
    b. ( )   cleaned
    c. ( )   placed on the shelf

4. Miniskirts *came out* in the 1960's.

    a. ( )   became popular
    b. ( )   became available to the public
    c. ( )   went out of style

5. In the 1930's, padded shoulders first *came in.*

    a. ( )   became fashionable
    b. ( )   became available to the public
    c. ( )   went out of style

6. Platform shoes *went out of fashion* quickly.

    a. ( )   became fashionable
    b. ( )   stopped being fashionable
    c. ( )   broke

7. If you have a good figure, you can *put on* anything and look great.

    a. ( )   get dressed in
    b. ( )   buy
    c. ( )   sew

8. If you *pull* a sweater *on* over your T-shirt, you will be warm enough.

    a. ( )   stretch
    b. ( )   get dressed in quickly
    c. ( )   remove

9. We *rolled up* our pants and walked into the lake.

        a. ( ) folded
        b. ( ) removed
        c. ( ) raised by rolling

10. When you enter a Japanese home you must *take off* your shoes.

        a. ( ) wear
        b. ( ) remove
        c. ( ) brush

11. Everyone was surprised when the president *showed up in* blue jeans.

        a. ( ) bought
        b. ( ) displayed
        c. ( ) appeared wearing

12. The little girl likes to *dress up*.

        a. ( ) put on formal clothes
        b. ( ) wear jeans and sneakers
        c. ( ) wear dirty dresses

13. She gained so much weight that she can't *zip up* her pants.

        a. ( ) wear
        b. ( ) remove
        c. ( ) close the zipper of

14. That tie doesn't *go with* your shirt.

        a. ( ) look good with
        b. ( ) look better than
        c. ( ) cover

15. She reads all the fashion magazines to *keep up with the times*.

        a. ( ) enjoy herself
        b. ( ) know what is new
        c. ( ) waste time

16.   Natural fabrics like cotton and silk *are* always *in vogue.*

a. ( )   are comfortable
b. ( )   are expensive
c. ( )   are fashionable

II. WORD ASSOCIATION

DIRECTIONS: Two of the three choices below can be used with the idiom. Mark the *two* answers that can be used to complete each sentence correctly.

1.   The seamstress came up with _____.

a. ( )   a solution to the problem
b. ( )   a logical explanation
c. ( )   a sewing machine

2.   The ten-foot sculpture was made out of_____.

a. ( )   junk
b. ( )   a chisel
c. ( )   coat hangers

3.   If you put the _____ together, it will look like new.

a. ( )   fragments
b. ( )   parts
c. ( )   piece

4.   _____ is coming out this year.

a. ( )   Last year's style
b. ( )   His autobiography
c. ( )   A new look

5.   _____ came in this spring.

a. ( )   Costume jewelry
b. ( )   Long hair
c. ( )   A new boutique

6. _____ have gone out of fashion before.

        a. ( ) Pointy-toed shoes
        b. ( ) Cuff links
        c. ( ) Clothes

7. Why don't you put on _____?

        a. ( ) your glasses
        b. ( ) your necklace
        c. ( ) your comb and brush

8. Please, take off _____ and make yourself at home.

        a. ( ) your shoes
        b. ( ) your coat
        c. ( ) your briefcase

9. One of the designer's models showed up in _____.

        a. ( ) another designer's dress
        b. ( ) a new pocketbook
        c. ( ) glasses

10. She pulled on _____.

        a. ( ) the three-thousand-dollar evening gown
        b. ( ) her bathing suit
        c. ( ) a pair of jeans and a turtleneck sweater

11. If it gets too hot you can roll up _____.

        a. ( ) your sleeves
        b. ( ) your shirt
        c. ( ) your pants

12. That _____ doesn't go with your skirt.

        a. ( ) blazer
        b. ( ) straight skirt
        c. ( ) lace blouse

13. He _____ to keep up with the times.

       a. ( ) goes shopping once a month
       b. ( ) reads a lot of magazines
       c. ( ) reads the encyclopedia

14. We have to dress up for _____.

       a. ( ) the reception
       b. ( ) the wedding gown
       c. ( ) the opera

15. She zipped up the _____.

       a. ( ) ski jacket
       b. ( ) dress
       c. ( ) diaper

16. _____ is in vogue this year.

       a. ( ) Wool
       b. ( ) Fashion
       c. ( ) Casual wear

III. THE POSITION OF THE OBJECT

DIRECTIONS: Fill in *one* of the blanks (a or b) in each sentence with the object given in parentheses. *Three* of the sentences do not have objects. For those sentences, do not write anything.

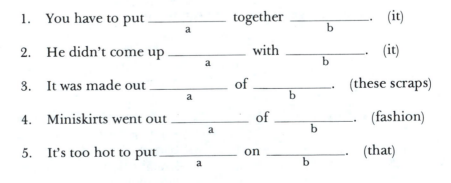

1. You have to put _____ together _____. (it)
               a   b

2. He didn't come up _____ with _____. (it)
                 a   b

3. It was made out _____ of _____. (these scraps)
              a   b

4. Miniskirts went out _____ of _____. (fashion)
               a   b

5. It's too hot to put _____ on _____. (that)
             a   b

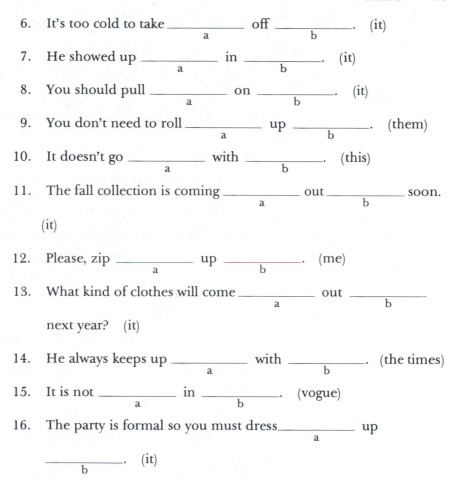

6. It's too cold to take _____ off _____.   (it)
                          a   b

7. He showed up _____ in _____.   (it)
                  a   b

8. You should pull _____ on _____.   (it)
                    a   b

9. You don't need to roll _____ up _____.   (them)
                           a   b

10. It doesn't go _____ with _____.   (this)
                   a   b

11. The fall collection is coming _____ out _____ soon.
                                   a   b

    (it)

12. Please, zip _____ up _____.   (me)
                 a   b

13. What kind of clothes will come _____ out _____
                                    a   b

    next year?   (it)

14. He always keeps up _____ with _____.   (the times)
                        a   b

15. It is not _____ in _____.   (vogue)
               a   b

16. The party is formal so you must dress_____ up
                                          a

    _____.   (it)
     b

IV. LISTENING COMPREHENSION ANSWER SHEET

DIRECTIONS: You will hear a situation presented in one or two sentences. Listen to each statement and mark the response that most closely corresponds to the situation.

1. a. ( ) The First Lady went to her husband's inauguration with the designer Halston.

   b. ( ) The First Lady wore a Halston hat to the inauguration.

   c. ( ) The President's wife designed a pillbox.

2. a. ( ) Short skirts were popular before 1920.

    b. ( ) Shirts became popular in the 1920's.

    c. ( ) The first time short skirts became fashionable was in the 1920's.

3. a. ( ) Minis, midis, and maxis were not fashionable in the 1960's.

    b. ( ) The 1960's was a time of changing hemlines.

    c. ( ) The mini was the only fashionable skirt in the 1960's.

4. a. ( ) Don't buy them if they are over one hundred dollars.

    b. ( ) Buy them if they look good with your dress.

    c. ( ) Buy them if they cost only $110.

5. a. ( ) She reads *The New York Times*.

    b. ( ) She works in Paris.

    c. ( ) It is necessary for her to know what is fashionable.

6. a. ( ) She was wearing an attractive outfit when she went to the store.

    b. ( ) She looked better in her own dress.

    c. ( ) She looked better in the outfit in the store.

7. a. ( ) That suit became popular last year.

    b. ( ) That suit became popular this year.

    c. ( ) That suit went out of fashion last year.

8. a. ( ) She sews them by hand.

    b. ( ) She doesn't buy pants that are too long for her.

    c. ( ) She makes them shorter by turning up the bottom.

9. a. ( ) His ties are fashionable now.

    b. ( ) His ties never went out of fashion.

    c. ( ) He expects his ties to be fashionable again.

10. a. ( ) They have metal taps.

 b. ( ) They are very stiff.

 c. ( ) They are very comfortable.

11. a. ( ) American fashion designers wear only casual clothes.

 b. ( ) American fashion designers would probably put an informal blouse with a very formal skirt.

 c. ( ) American fashions are generally informal and comfortable.

12. a. ( ) The pants were too loose.

 b. ( ) The pants were too tight.

 c. ( ) The zipper was broken.

13. a. ( ) She must be very careful with support pantyhose.

 b. ( ) She prefers sheer pantyhose.

 c. ( ) She probably wears support pantyhose.

14. a. ( ) Peter was in a tuxedo.

 b. ( ) Peter was in a pair of jeans.

 c. ( ) Peter didn't go to the birthday party.

15. a. ( ) The new designer was very innovative.

 b. ( ) The new designer created many designs.

 c. ( ) The new designer didn't produce anything original.

V. FILL IN

DIRECTIONS: Fill in the blanks with the correct preposition or particle.

It happened during the California Gold Rush. An American sailmaker moved to the West Coast with a large supply of blue canvas and orange thread. His name was Levi Strauss.

Strauss had a problem in California. Nobody wanted to buy his supplies; everybody was too busy digging for gold. "Gold diggers don't need sails," he thought, "they need strong trousers." So Strauss came up _____ a clever idea—to make trousers for the gold diggers
1
_____ of his material.
2

He hired a saddlemaker and they put _____ the blue canvas,
3
the orange thread, and copper rivets to produce the strongest trousers ever made. In 1850, the first blue jeans came _____.
4

Once they came _____, Levi's never went _____. [c]
5   6
fashion. Workmen put them _____; children pull them
7
_____ and roll them _____; cowboys never take them
8   9
_____; even presidents show _____ in them.
10   11

Americans, in general, don't like to dress _____. They pre-
12
fer to wear a pair of jeans which they can zip _____ in a second.
13
Jeans go _____ everything—a sweatshirt or a mink coat. People
14
who keep up _____ the times buy designer jeans. All over the
15
world jeans are _____ vogue.
16

Levi Strauss didn't need to dig for gold; his invention was a gold mine.

VI. ADDITIONAL EXERCISES

1. Make up a story about the picture at the beginning of the chapter. Use as many idioms as possible. This exercise can be written or oral.
2. Ask each other questions about the picture. You must use an idiom in your response.
3. Use the lines below the picture for a dictation exercise. The teacher or a student dictates the introductory passage and the students write it.
4. Rewrite the introductory passage in the future tense.

7

ANGER

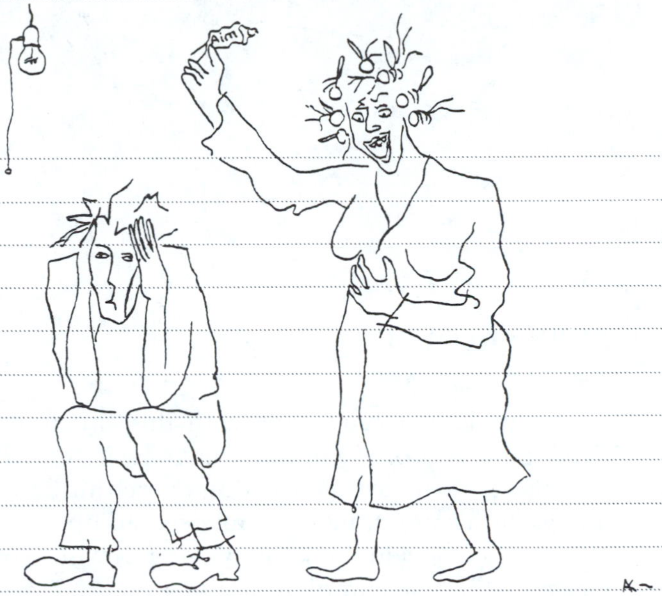
Aim

Anger

INTRODUCTORY PASSAGE

This is it! I can't **cope with** this situation any longer. You are **driving** me **out of my mind.** You know it **gets on my nerves,** but you continue to do it anyway. You **don't** even **think twice about** what you're doing. At this point, I **am** completely **fed up.**

Of course, you think I'm **picking on** you. You're sure I'm looking for something to **complain about** because I **got out of bed on the wrong side.** Well, you're wrong.

Are you deaf? I'm talking to you! Why are you looking at me like that? Why do you always **hold** everything **in?** Why don't you say something? Let's **have** it **out** right now, or don't you **feel like** discussing it?

Listen, do you really think I am going to **put up with** this forever? Oh, no. I won't **stand for** it.

This is it! I have to **calm down.** I am **not** going to **lose any** more **sleep over** it. You have to **cut it out,** that's all. I don't **object to** your affairs, but I'm telling you for the last time, don't squeeze the toothpaste in the middle!

NOTES

IDIOMS AND THE POSITION OF THEIR OBJECTS	GRAMMATICAL NOTES	STYLE
1. cope with [ ] _____		
2. drive [ ] out of [his/her mind] _____		

100

3. get on   [one's nerves]   _____

_____

4. (not) think twice about   [   ]   _____

_____

5. be fed up   _____   informal

_____

6. pick on   [   ]   _____   informal

_____

7. complain about   [   ]   _____

_____

8. get out of   [bed]   on   [the wrong side]   _____   informal

_____

9. hold   [   ]   in   _____

_____

10. have   [   ]   out   _____   informal

_____

11. feel like   [   ]   _____ object is usually the *-ing* form _____

_____

12. put up with   [   ]   _____ often negative _____   informal

_____

13. stand for [   ] _____ usually negative _____ informal

_____

14. calm [   ] down _____ object can be omitted _____

_____

15. (not) lose [any sleep] over [   ] _____ informal

_____

16. cut [   ] out _____

_____

17. object to [   ] _____

_____

Use this page for one or more of the following exercises:

- Write the meaning of the idiom.
- Write sample sentences.
- Look for the idioms in short stories, novels, newspapers, or magazines, and copy the sentences containing them.
- Give examples of appropriate direct objects or objects of the preposition for each idiom that requires an object.
- Practice saying the idioms with correct stress. In general, verbs and particles are stressed, but prepositions are unstressed.

I. DEFINITIONS

DIRECTIONS: Mark the answer that is the closest synonym for the italicized idioms.

1. He quit his job because he couldn't *cope with* all the pressure.

       a. (   ) overcome
       b. (   ) avoid
       c. (   ) enjoy

2. His constant complaining is *driving me out of my mind.*

    a. ( ) annoying me a little
    b. ( ) too loud
    c. ( ) making me very nervous

3. Her high-pitched voice *gets on everybody's nerves.*

    a. ( ) sounds nervous
    b. ( ) irritates everybody
    c. ( ) sounds melodious

4. She *didn't think twice about* selling drugs.

    a. ( ) didn't want to get involved in
    b. ( ) couldn't imagine
    c. ( ) didn't worry about

5. We're *fed up* with the weather here.

    a. ( ) enjoying
    b. ( ) tired of
    c. ( ) pleased with

6. He always *picks on* his little brother.

    a. ( ) chooses for teasing or punishment
    b. ( ) lifts
    c. ( ) beats

7. You are always *complaining about* your salary.

    a. ( ) discussing
    b. ( ) expressing a negative opinion about
    c. ( ) worrying about

8. It's better not to talk to him. He *got out of bed on the wrong side* this morning.

    a. ( ) was in a bad mood when he went to sleep
    b. ( ) hurt himself when he got up
    c. ( ) has been in a bad mood since he got up

9. If you are angry, tell me. Don't *hold* it *in*.

    a. ( )   keep it inside
    b. ( )   explain why
    c. ( )   be embarrassed

10. They were both angry at each other and finally they *had* it *out*.

    a. ( )   got divorced
    b. ( )   settled a problem by discussing it angrily and freely
    c. ( )   became friends again

11. I don't *feel like* going out in the rain. Let's stay home.

    a. ( )   want to
    b. ( )   feel well enough to
    c. ( )   enjoy

12. His secretary can't *put up with* his bad manners anymore.

    a. ( )   tolerate
    b. ( )   try to change
    c. ( )   ignore

13. The teacher wouldn't *stand for* any cheating during the exam.

    a. ( )   tolerate
    b. ( )   stop
    c. ( )   ignore

14. If you want to discuss the matter, you must *calm down* first.

    a. ( )   become quiet, more relaxed
    b. ( )   make an appointment
    c. ( )   explain your position

15. I would*n't lose any sleep over* the news if I were you.

    a. ( )   not listen to
    b. ( )   not discuss
    c. ( )   not worry about

16. If you don't *cut out* smoking three packs of cigarettes a day, you will die before you are fifty.

   a. ( ) think about
   b. ( ) stop
   c. ( ) limit yourself to

17. The cleaning lady *objected to* washing windows.

   a. ( ) avoided
   b. ( ) liked
   c. ( ) expressed a negative attitude about

II. WORD ASSOCIATION

DIRECTIONS: Two of the three choices below can be used with the idiom. Mark the *two* answers that can be used to complete each sentence correctly.

1. It was extremely difficult for her to cope with _____.

   a. ( ) the crisis
   b. ( ) her husband's death
   c. ( ) the clock

2. _____ is driving him out of his mind.

   a. ( ) The constant noise
   b. ( ) His brain
   c. ( ) Her complaining

3. _____ gets on her nerves.

   a. ( ) Driving to work
   b. ( ) Rock 'n roll
   c. ( ) Tension

4. He didn't think twice about _____.

    a. (   )   reading
    b. (   )   betraying his colleague
    c. (   )   recommending her for the job

5. _____ is fed up.

    a. (   )   The mayor
    b. (   )   Her husband
    c. (   )   Her job

6. Why do you always pick on _____?

    a. (   )   that little boy
    b. (   )   the bus
    c. (   )   your younger sister

7. Nobody wants to listen to you complain about _____.

    a. (   )   your great boss
    b. (   )   your salary
    c. (   )   being fired

8. I think _____ got out of bed on the wrong side today.

    a. (   )   my supervisor
    b. (   )   that girl with the smile on her face
    c. (   )   my sister

9. In some countries people must hold in their _____.

    a. (   )   emotions
    b. (   )   anger
    c. (   )   mistakes

10. _____ had it out last night.

    a. (   )   Her parents
    b. (   )   The angry customer
    c. (   )   Two of the soccer players

11.   He doesn't feel like _____.

       a.   ( )   study
       b.   ( )   asking her to go to the party
       c.   ( )   playing tennis

12.   She can't put up with _____.

       a.   ( )   her in-laws
       b.   ( )   her favorite music
       c.   ( )   the air pollution here

13.   We won't stand for _____.

       a.   ( )   any discrimination
       b.   ( )   such terrible working conditions
       c.   ( )   anybody

14.   She couldn't calm down after _____.

       a.   ( )   the robbery
       b.   ( )   the premiere
       c.   ( )   taking a walk

15.   I can see you didn't lose any sleep over _____.

       a.   ( )   your breakfast
       b.   ( )   the scandal
       c.   ( )   the news of his arrest

16.   The doctor told her to cut out _____.

       a.   ( )   smoking
       b.   ( )   alcoholic beverages
       c.   ( )   sleeping

17.   He always objects to _____.

       a.   ( )   delicious food
       b.   ( )   having to stay overtime
       c.   ( )   being interrupted

III. THE POSITION OF THE OBJECT

DIRECTIONS: Fill in *one* of the blanks (a or b) in each sentence with the object given in parentheses. *One* of the sentences does not have an object. For that sentence, do not write anything.

1. You should calm _____ down _____. (him)
   a   b

2. We can't cope _____ with _____. (it)
   a   b

3. The hammering is getting _____ on _____. (his nerves)
   a   b

4. He didn't think twice _____ about _____. (it)
   a   b

5. You shouldn't pick _____ on _____. (him)
   a   b

6. You are always complaining _____ about _____. (it)
   a   b

7. Don't hold _____ in _____. (it)
   a   b

8. It is time to have _____ out _____. (it)
   a   b

9. We don't feel _____ like _____. (it)
   a   b

10. She won't put up _____ with _____. (it)
    a   b

11. They aren't going to stand _____ for _____. (it)
    a   b

12. She didn't lose any sleep _____ over _____. (it)
    a   b

13. He is totally fed _____ up _____. (it)
    a   b

14. You must cut _____ out _____. (it)
    a   b

15. He doesn't object _____ to _____. (it)
    a   b

16. You are driving _____ out _____ of my mind. (me)
    a   b

17. He got out _____ of _____ on the wrong side. (bed)
    a   b

IV. LISTENING COMPREHENSION ANSWER SHEET

DIRECTIONS: You will hear a short dialogue followed by a question. After you hear each question, read the three choices and mark the response that answers the question correctly.

1. a. ( ) She feels a little sick.
    b. ( ) She never likes to go to parties.
    c. ( ) She doesn't want to go.

2. a. ( ) She was going out.
    b. ( ) She was yelling at the man.
    c. ( ) She was checking into a hotel.

3. a. ( ) He calmed down immediately.
    b. ( ) He became extremely angry.
    c. ( ) He didn't care.

4. a. ( ) All of them disagreed with him.
    b. ( ) Some of them disagreed with him.
    c. ( ) There was no reaction.

5. a. ( ) He exploded.
    b. ( ) He wanted to control himself but couldn't.
    c. ( ) He wanted to scream but controlled himself.

6. a. ( ) "I'm angry."
    b. ( ) "Don't tease me."
    c. ( ) "You look like an elephant in that dress."

7. a. ( ) Most of them liked it because it was so tall.
    b. ( ) They wanted something taller than 300 meters.
    c. ( ) It bothered their sense of beauty.

8. a. ( ) The doctor was lying on the couch.
    b. ( ) The doctor was talking all the time.
    c. ( ) The patient was nervous because the doctor didn't say anything.

9. a. ( ) He was not very worried.

    b. ( ) It was so terrible that he couldn't sleep.

    c. ( ) He already lost a lot of sleep over it.

10. a. ( ) It didn't bother him.

     b. ( ) He became very upset.

     c. ( ) He asked her for a divorce.

11. a. ( ) They don't want to discuss it.

     b. ( ) They would say it's impossible.

     c. ( ) It doesn't bother them at all.

12. a. ( ) She was able to accept it.

     b. ( ) She became depressed.

     c. ( ) She became extremely angry.

13. a. ( ) He will stop being a back-seat driver if the woman is more polite with him.

     b. ( ) He will not stop being a back-seat driver.

     c. ( ) He won't stand for any back-seat drivers in the car.

14. a. ( ) Her husband doesn't want to discuss it.

     b. ( ) She will not feel better after discussing it.

     c. ( ) Her husband will lose control during the fight.

15. a. ( ) He has been in a bad mood since he got up.

     b. ( ) The weather affected him.

     c. ( ) He doesn't like to talk to people.

V. FILL IN

DIRECTIONS: Fill in the blanks with the correct preposition or particle.

This is it! I can't cope _____ this situation any longer. You
1

are driving me _____ of my mind. You know it gets _____
2   3

my nerves, but you continue to do it anyway. You don't even think twice

_____ what you're doing. At this point, I am completely fed
   4

_____ .
  5

Of course, you think I'm picking _____ you. You're sure I'm
      6

looking for something to complain _____ because I got out
       7

_____ bed on the wrong side. Well, you're wrong.
  8

Are you deaf? I'm talking to you! Why are you looking at me like

that? Why do you always hold everything _____ ? Why don't you
       9

say something? Let's have it _____ right now, or don't you
      10

feel _____ discussing it?
   11

Listen, do you really think I am going to put _____ with this
      12

forever? Oh, no. I won't stand _____ it.
     13

This is it! I have to calm _____ . I am not going to lose any
     14

more sleep _____ it. You have to cut it _____ , that's all. I
    15   16

don't object _____ your affairs, but I'm telling you for the last
    17

time, don't squeeze the toothpaste in the middle!

ADDITIONAL EXERCISES

1. Make up a story about the picture at the beginning of the chapter. Use as many idioms as possible. This exercise can be written or oral.
2. Ask each other questions about the picture. You must use an idiom in your response.
3. Use the lines below the picture for a dictation exercise. The teacher or a student dictates the introductory passage and the students write it.
4. Rewrite the introductory passage in the past tense.

8

TRAVEL

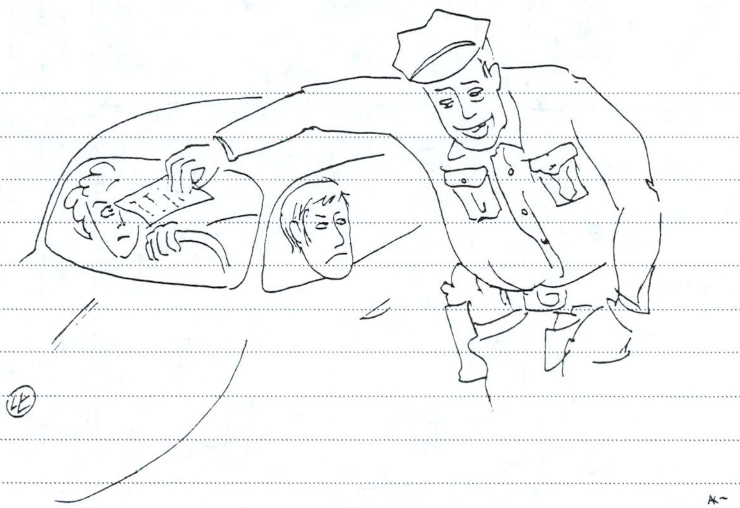

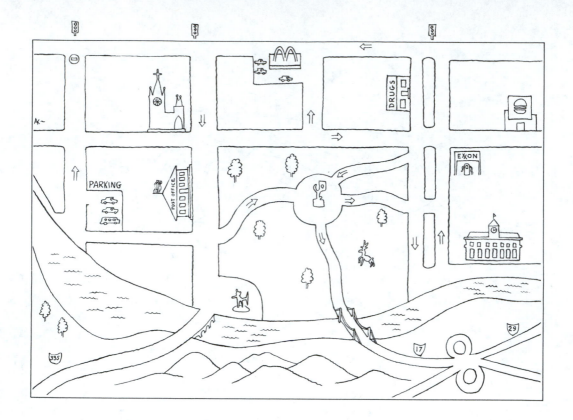

Travel

INTRODUCTORY PASSAGE

DIRECTIONS: Read the paragraph below and draw the route on the map.

Start out at the parking lot behind the Post Office. **Back** the car **up** and turn right when you leave the lot. Make a right at the corner. You'll **pass by** a church. Keep going. Make a left at the next corner. **Pull into** the parking lot. You can get something to eat there. **Pull out of** the lot on the other street and turn left at the light. Go straight ahead. **Pull over** in front of the Post Office to mail a package, then **get into** the left lane and **cut across** the park. When you **get to** the circle, make the second right. Make a left when you leave the park. If you need gas, **fill up** your tank at the corner. Continue along the same street and **turn around** at the traffic light. **Stop off** at the drugstore. Then **go back to** the park, go around the monument, and **head for** the bridge. Don't **run over** any deer. The bridge will take you to Route 17. You can **make good time** on 17.

(⇒ indicates the direction of the traffic)

NOTES

IDIOMS AND THE POSITION
OF THEIR OBJECTS   *GRAMMATICAL NOTES*   *STYLE*

1. start out _____

2. back [   ] up _____ object can be omitted _____

3. pass by [   ] _____

4. pull into [   ] _____ object is usually a noun _____

5. pull out of [   ] _____ object is usually a noun ____ _____

6. pull [   ] over _____ object can be omitted _____

7. get into [   ] _____

8. cut across [   ] _____ object is usually a noun _____

9. get to [   ] _____

10. fill [   ] up _____ informal

_____

11. turn [   ] around ____object can be omitted_____

_____

12. stop off _____

_____

13. go back to [   ] ____object is usually a noun_____

_____

14. head for [   ] _____ informal

_____

15. run [   ] over _____

_____

16. make [good time] _____

_____

Use this page for one or more of the following exercises:

- Write the meaning of the idiom.
- Write sample sentences.
- Look for the idioms in short stories, novels, newspapers, or magazines, and copy the sentences containing them.
- Give examples of appropriate direct objects or objects of the preposition for each idiom that requires an object.
- Practice saying the idioms with correct stress. In general, verbs and particles are stressed, but prepositions are unstressed.

I. DEFINITIONS

DIRECTIONS: Mark the answer that is the closest synonym for the italicized idioms.

1. The runners *started out* at one end of the city and finished at the other end.

    a. ( ) stopped
    b. ( ) ended
    c. ( ) began

2. During his road test he had to *back up* while he was parking.

    a. ( ) fix the mirror
    b. ( ) go forward
    c. ( ) go in reverse

3. The bus *passes by* her house every fifteen minutes.

    a. ( ) goes near
    b. ( ) goes past
    c. ( ) stops at

4. If you need gas you had better *pull into* the next gas station.

    a. ( ) get it at
    b. ( ) look for
    c. ( ) move closer to and enter

5. The train *pulled out of* the station two minutes early.

    a. ( ) left
    b. ( ) moved closer to
    c. ( ) stopped at

6. The policeman told her to *pull over*.

    a. ( ) stop immediately
    b. ( ) move to the side of the road and stop
    c. ( ) drive slowly

7. If you don't *get into* the right lane you won't be able to turn right at the corner.

    a. ( ) enter
    b. ( ) avoid
    c. ( ) pass the cars in

8. The children always *cut across* the park to go to the ice cream parlor.

        a. ( ) take a shorter route through
        b. ( ) go around
        c. ( ) prefer

9. When you *get to* the hotel, call us collect.

        a. ( ) see
        b. ( ) arrive at
        c. ( ) leave

10. We should *fill up* the tank before we reach the highway.

        a. ( ) fix
        b. ( ) make completely full
        c. ( ) put a little gas in

11. He got lost so he *turned around* and went to the nearest gas station for directions.

        a. ( ) continued in the same direction
        b. ( ) went in the opposite direction
        c. ( ) looked at the map

12. When he *stopped off* at the candy store, he lost his wallet.

        a. ( ) stopped for something during a trip
        b. ( ) parked
        c. ( ) looked

13. She didn't want to *go back to* the scene of the accident.

        a. ( ) go in reverse to
        b. ( ) walk to
        c. ( ) return to

14. It is time to *head for* home.

        a. ( ) leave
        b. ( ) go in the direction of
        c. ( ) think about

15.   The drunken driver *ran over* the little poodle.

        a.   ( )   hit with a moving vehicle
        b.   ( )   followed
        c.   ( )   didn't see

16.   It usually takes an hour to get here. If you left home only forty-five minutes ago, you *made good time.*

        a.   ( )   enjoyed the trip
        b.   ( )   traveled at a good speed
        c.   ( )   drove much too fast

II. WORD ASSOCIATION

DIRECTIONS: Two of the three choices below can be used with the idiom. Mark the *two* answers that can be used to complete each sentence correctly.

1.   _____ started out at 14th Street.

        a.   ( )   The parade
        b.   ( )   His apartment
        c.   ( )   The runners

2.   Every morning the school bus passes by _____.

        a.   ( )   our door
        b.   ( )   the house
        c.   ( )   the wind

3.   We're going to pull into _____.

        a.   ( )   the store
        b.   ( )   the station
        c.   ( )   the parking lot

4.   He pulled out of _____ in a hurry.

a. (   )   the garage
b. (   )   the stoplight
c. (   )   the parking space

5. The policeman told the _____ to pull over.

a. (   )   taxi driver
b. (   )   bus
c. (   )   reckless driver

6. He had trouble backing _____ up.

a. (   )   the station wagon
b. (   )   reverse
c. (   )   the truck

7. It was impossible to get into _____.

a. (   )   the left lane
b. (   )   the side of the road
c. (   )   the parking space

8. We always cut across _____ on the way to school.

a. (   )   the parking lot
b. (   )   the playground
c. (   )   the trees

9. They didn't get to _____ until 1:00 A.M.

a. (   )   their trip
b. (   )   their destination
c. (   )   the fork in the road

10. Let's go to the gas station and have the _____ filled up.

a. (   )   gas pump
b. (   )   car
c. (   )   tank

11.   Before going to the party we had to stop off _____.

                            a.   ( )   at the hospital to visit a friend
                            b.   ( )   for wine
                            c.   ( )   the highway

12.   You must turn _____ around immediately!

                            a.   ( )   the plane
                            b.   ( )   the car
                            c.   ( )   the street

13.   She had to go back to _____.

                            a.   ( )   a checkup
                            b.   ( )   the supermarket
                            c.   ( )   the car

14.   Right now they are headed for _____.

                            a.   ( )   trouble
                            b.   ( )   school
                            c.   ( )   this afternoon

15.   The bus driver ran over _____.

                            a.   ( )   a car
                            b.   ( )   a pedestrian
                            c.   ( )   a squirrel

16.   _____ made good time today.

                            a.   ( )   The chauffeur
                            b.   ( )   The train
                            c.   ( )   The clock

III. THE POSITION OF THE OBJECT

DIRECTIONS: Fill in *one* of the blanks (a or b) in each sentence with the object given in parentheses. *Three* of the sentences do not have objects. For those sentences, do not write anything.

1. You can pull _____ into _____. (the lot)
   _a _b

2. He pulled out _____ of _____. (the driveway)
   _a _b

3. Please pull _____ over _____. (the car)
   _a _b

4. He can't back _____ up _____. (it)
   _a _b

5. She passes _____ by _____ at 8:45. (the house)
   _a _b

6. It wasn't easy to get _____ into _____. (it)
   _a _b

7. He wanted to cut _____ across _____. (the park)
   _a _b

8. In a little while we will get _____ to _____.
   _a _b

   (our stop)

9. It's a long trip. We should start _____ out _____
   _a _b

   early.   (it)

10. Every week she has to fill _____ up _____. (it)
    _a _b

11. It isn't difficult to turn _____ around _____. (it)
    _a _b

12. Let's stop _____ off _____ at the store.   (it)
    _a _b

13. You're twenty minutes early! You really made _____ good
    _a

    time _____.   (it)
    _b

14. We had to go back _____ to _____. (the house)
    _a _b

15. He headed _____ for _____.   (the shopping
    _a _b

    center)

16. The teenager ran _____ over _____. (him)
    _a _b

IV. LISTENING COMPREHENSION ANSWER SHEET

DIRECTIONS: Most of the questions in this exercise are about the plan of the city given below. Listen to each question, look at the plan, and mark the response that answers the question correctly.

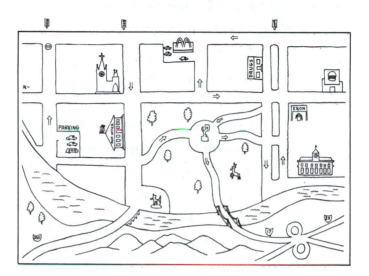

1. a. ( ) Turn around in the park.
    b. ( ) Cut across the park.
    c. ( ) Pass by the drugstore.

2. a. ( ) Cut across the street.
    b. ( ) Turn around.
    c. ( ) Turn right.

3. a. ( ) Back up.
    b. ( ) Head for Route 17.
    c. ( ) Run over something.

4. a. ( ) In the park.
    b. ( ) In the parking lot.
    c. ( ) At the gas station.

5. a. ( ) Route 29.

    b. ( ) A bridge.

    c. ( ) The monument.

6. a. ( ) Stop off at the restaurant.

    b. ( ) Head for the post office.

    c. ( ) Fill up the tank.

7. a. ( ) Go around the circle.

    b. ( ) Take Route 17.

    c. ( ) Drive near the post office or the gas station.

8. a. ( ) You will be going the wrong way.

    b. ( ) You will be going the right way.

    c. ( ) You will make good time.

9. a. ( ) Head for Route 335.

    b. ( ) Run him over.

    c. ( ) Pull over.

10. a. ( ) Cut across the park.

    b. ( ) Go through the park, make a left when you leave the park, and make another left at the traffic light, then another left at the next traffic light.

    c. ( ) Walk.

V. FILL IN

DIRECTIONS: Fill in the blanks with the correct preposition or particle. (Note: Number 16 requires a noun.)

Start _____ at the parking lot behind the Post Office. Back
           1

the car_____ and turn right when you leave the lot. Make a right
          2

at the corner. You'll pass _____ a church. Keep going. Make a
                            3

left at the next corner. Pull _____ the parking lot. You can get
                              4

something to eat there. Pull _____ of the lot on the other street
                            5

and turn left at the light. Go straight ahead. Pull _____ in front of
                                                    6

the Post Office to mail a package, then get _____ the left lane and
                                            7

cut _____ the park. When you get _____ the circle, make
        8   9

the second right. Make a left when you leave the park. If you need gas,

fill _____ your tank at the corner. Continue along the same street
        10

and turn _____ at the traffic light. Stop _____ at the
            11   12

drugstore. Then go _____ to the park, go around the monument,
                      13

and head _____ the bridge. Don't run _____ any deer.
            14   15

The bridge will take you to Route 17. You can make good _____
                                                          16

on 17.

VI. PRACTICAL APPLICATION

DIRECTIONS: Look at the Report of Road Test below. As you can see, Paul Otis failed the test. The reasons for failure are marked. Use the reasons for failure and the idioms in parentheses to make up sentences explaining what Paul did wrong.

REPORT OF ROAD TEST – CLASS 4, 5, & 6

Applicant's Signature	Paul Otis			Date of Birth	2-14-52
Validation No.	2686129	MV-285 ☐ attached	Post 4		
Year & Make	79 Ford	Plate No. 698 XEY		Comm'l. School ☐ Vehicle ☐	Test Date 1-24-81
Signature of Motor Vehicle License Inspector	J. Robertson			Shield No.	531

REASONS FOR FAILURE IN ROAD TEST

GROUNDS FOR IMMEDIATE FAILURE

☐ Accident   ☐ Dangerous Action   ☐ Serious Viol.   ☐ 2 Ten Point Items

Reason

☑ MISCELLANEOUS GRADED REASONS (More than 20 points circled below)

A. LEAVING CURB
1. Fails to ☐ Observe ☑ Signal
   ☐ On time ☐ Adequately   (5)
2. Uses mirror only   (4)

B. TURNING & INTERSECTIONS
3. Fails to signal for turns   5
4. Fails to signal properly   5
5. Fails to get in proper lane for turn   5
6. Excessive speed ☐ Turns
   ☐ Intersections   5
7. Fails to stop near center of intersection
   when waiting to make left turn   5
8. Turns wide - short right   3
9. Turns wide - short left   3
10. Poor judgment approaching or at
    intersections ☐ Speed
    ☐ Turning ☐ Stopping
    ☐ Observing   5

C. PARKING, BACKING & U-TURN
11. Fails to signal   (5)
12. Fails to adequately observe or
    use caution   5
13. Unable to park properly   10
14. Unable to make U-turn   10
15. Excessive space for parking   (3)
16. Excessive maneuvers in
    ☑ U-turn ☐ Parking   (3)
17. Parks too far from curb   3

D. TRAFFIC DRIVING
18. Fails to keep right   5
19. Improper lane of traffic   (5)
20. Follows too closely   5
21. Speed excessive for conditions
    ☐ Traffic ☐ Weather ☐ Road   10
22. Fails to yield right of way to
    ☑ Pedestrian ☐ Other   (10)
23. Poor judgment in traffic   5
24. When changing lanes, fails to
    ☐ Observe ☐ Signal ☐ Use caution   5
25. Fails to anticipate actions of
    ☐ Pedestrian ☐ Other   5
26. Fails to anticipate potential hazards   5

E. GENERAL
27. Repeated stalling   5
28. Poor engine control   5
29. Poor steering control ☐ Turning
    ☐ Straight driving ☑ Maneuvers   10
30. Delayed braking   5
31. Abrupt braking   5
32. Poor use of gears
    ☐ Automatic ☐ Standard   5
33. Poor clutch control   3
34. Rolling on grade   5
35. Too slow ☐ Intersections ☐ Turns
    ☐ Maneuvers ☐ Traffic driving   5
36. Poor reaction to emergencies   5
37. Inattentive to traffic
    ☐ Signs ☐ Signals   5

☐ PASSED	☑ FAILED		TOTAL	34

1. (start out) _____

_____

2. (pull out of) _____

_____

3. (pull into) _____

_____

4. (back up) _____

_____

5. (turn around) _____

_____

6. (get into) _____

_____

7. (run over) _____

_____

VII. ADDITIONAL EXERCISES

1. Make up a story about the picture at the beginning of the chapter. Use as many idioms as possible. This exercise can be written or oral.
2. Ask each other questions about the picture. You must use an idiom in your response.
3. Use the lines below the picture for a dictation exercise. The teacher or a student dictates the introductory passage and the students write it.
4. Rewrite the introductory passage in the first person singular (I) and change each verb to the past tense.

9

TAKE IT EASY

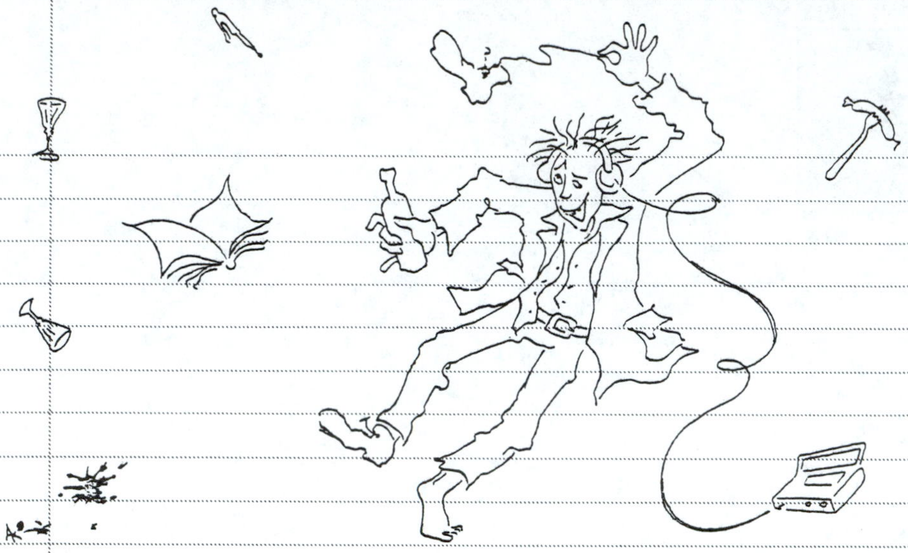

Take It Easy

INTRODUCTORY PASSAGE

For some people, learning English is hard work, but other people know how to **take it easy.** They have a lot of fun because they **liven up** their studies. Here are some tips from students of different nationalities:

French	—	**Take** an American girl **out** and forget the language barrier.
Spanish	—	**Drop by** a friend's house and **stay up** all night dancing to rock 'n roll. Use American body language.
Germans	—	Organize a group, **skim through** your guidebook, and hire an interpreter to **show** you **around.**
Iranians	—	**Put your feet up** and go to sleep with your textbook under your pillow.
Russians	—	**Have** a few Americans **over** for dinner. You will forget your pronunciation problem after the third bottle of vodka.
Japanese	—	**Turn on** the radio, **switch on** the TV, **plug in** the headphones, and **bury yourself in** your dictionary.

NOTES

IDIOMS AND THE POSITION OF THEIR OBJECTS	*GRAMMATICAL NOTES*	*STYLE*
1. take [it] easy	often imperative	informal

129

2. liven [   ] up _____   informal

    _____

3. take [   ] out _____

    _____

4. drop by _____   informal

    _____

5. stay up _____

    _____

6. skim through [   ] _____

    _____

7. show [   ] around _____

    _____

8. put [one's feet] up _____   informal

    _____

9. have [   ] over _____

    _____

10. turn [   ] on _____

    _____

11. switch [   ] on _____   informal

    _____

12. plug [   ] in _____

_____

13. bury [oneself] in [   ] _____

_____

Use this page for one or more of the following exercises:

- Write the meaning of the idiom.
- Write sample sentences.
- Look for the idioms in short stories, novels, newspapers, or magazines, and copy the sentences containing them.
- Give examples of appropriate direct objects or objects of the preposition for each idiom that requires an object.
- Practice saying the idioms with correct stress. In general, verbs and particles are stressed, but prepositions are unstressed.

I. DEFINITIONS

DIRECTIONS: Mark the answer that is the closest synonym for the italicized idioms.

1. *Take it easy,* dinner will be ready in a few minutes.

      a. ( ) hurry
      b. ( ) relax, be calm
      c. ( ) come here

2. The party was boring until one girl started to do a belly dance. That *livened* things *up*.

      a. ( ) made more exciting
      b. ( ) took time
      c. ( ) made boring

3. She left him because he never *took* her *out.*

      a. ( ) visited
      b. ( ) invited for entertainment
      c. ( ) asked where she wanted to go

4. Why don't you *drop by* on your way home from work tonight.

        a. (   ) bring it to me
        b. (   ) visit informally
        c. (   ) come for a dinner party

5. The children *stayed up* all night on Christmas Eve.

        a. (   ) slept
        b. (   ) talked
        c. (   ) remained awake

6. It takes him too long to read novels in English so he usually *skims through* them.

        a. (   ) translates
        b. (   ) doesn't try to read
        c. (   ) reads quickly to get the general idea of

7. It was her first trip to Rome so she got a tour guide to *show* her *around*.

        a. (   ) take on a tour
        b. (   ) translate for
        c. (   ) introduce to people

8. Her husband had a hangover so he just *put his feet up* and watched TV all day.

        a. (   ) washed himself
        b. (   ) did exercise
        c. (   ) rested

9. We're *having* the whole class *over* for dinner tonight.

        a. (   ) inviting to the restaurant again
        b. (   ) going out with
        c. (   ) inviting to our home

10.   She is afraid of the dark so the minute she enters the house she *turns on* all the lights.

>   a.   ( )   touches a button to start
>   b.   ( )   looks for
>   c.   ( )   cleans

11.   He finally paid his gas and electric bill after three months and the company *switched on* the electricity this morning.

>   a.   ( )   touched a button to start
>   b.   ( )   stopped
>   c.   ( )   disconnected the power supply

12.   The alarm didn't ring because I forgot to *plug in* the clock-radio.

>   a.   ( )   put the plug in the socket
>   b.   ( )   pull the plug out of the socket
>   c.   ( )   set

13.   Every Sunday she *buries herself in* the crossword puzzle.

>   a.   ( )   finishes
>   b.   ( )   becomes very involved in
>   c.   ( )   tries to do

II. WORD ASSOCIATION

DIRECTIONS: Two of the three choices below can be used with the idiom. Mark the *two* answers that can be used to complete each sentence correctly.

1.   Take it easy, _____.

>   a.   ( )   you're working too hard
>   b.   ( )   you're making me nervous
>   c.   ( )   we have to finish in three minutes

2. Your jokes really livened up the _____.

    a. ( ) class
    b. ( ) book
    c. ( ) party

3. He's a good father. He takes _____ out every weekend.

    a. ( ) his children
    b. ( ) the movies
    c. ( ) the whole family

4. She was so nervous she stayed up all night _____.

    a. ( ) sleeping
    b. ( ) watching television
    c. ( ) talking to her roommate

5. _____ showed us around all morning.

    a. ( ) The tour guide
    b. ( ) The receptionist
    c. ( ) The guidebook

6. After _____ he came home, put his feet up, and had a drink.

    a. ( ) the seven-hour exam
    b. ( ) a ten-hour sleep
    c. ( ) working all night

7. We're having some friends over this weekend _____.

    a. ( ) for drinks
    b. ( ) for a barbeque
    c. ( ) to clean the house

8. She said to drop by _____ any morning.

    a. ( ) for class
    b. ( ) for a chat
    c. ( ) for a few minutes

9. You should at least skim through _____ before
    your exam.

    a. ( )   the chapter
    b. ( )   your notes
    c. ( )   each word

10. The little girl turned on _____.

    a. ( )   the light
    b. ( )   the stereo
    c. ( )   the watch

11. During the blackout, he tried to switch on the _____
    but nothing worked.

    a. ( )   lamp
    b. ( )   telephone
    c. ( )   radio

12. After the time he got an electric shock, he was afraid to plug in
    the _____.

    a. ( )   toaster
    b. ( )   on-off button
    c. ( )   sewing machine

13. As soon as he gets to the office, he always buries himself in
    _____.

    a. ( )   his paperwork
    b. ( )   the newspaper
    c. ( )   the cemetery

III. THE POSITION OF THE OBJECT

DIRECTIONS: Fill in *one* of the blanks (a or b) in each sentence with the
object given in parentheses. *Two* of the sentences do not have objects. For
those sentences, do not write anything.

1. You should learn to take _____a_____ easy _____b_____. (it)

2. He wanted to liven _____ up _____. (it)
   a   b

3. If you are free, please drop _____ by _____. (it)
   a   b

4. They are going to show _____ around _____. (us)
   a   b

5. She wants to have _____ over _____. (them)
   a   b

6. If you have a few minutes, skim _____ through
   a

   _____. (this)
   b

7. He didn't know how to turn _____ on _____. (it)
   a   b

8. He was so sleepy that he couldn't stay _____ up
   a

   _____. (it)
   b

9. She has buried herself _____ in _____. (it)
   a   b

10. Go to the living room and switch _____ on _____.
    a   b

   (it)

11. It's impossible to plug _____ in _____. (it)
    a   b

12. Now you can put _____ up _____. (your feet)
    a   b

13. She is going to take _____ out _____. (him)
    a   b

IV. LISTENING COMPREHENSION ANSWER SHEET

DIRECTIONS: You will hear a situation presented in one or two sentences. Listen to each statement and mark the response that most closely corresponds to the situation.

1. a. ( ) She was meeting friends at the club.
   b. ( ) She had to hurry home.
   c. ( ) Her friends didn't come to the club until 8:00.

2. a. ( ) He put his feet up during the party.

   b. ( ) He didn't do anything during the party.

   c. ( ) The next morning, he just relaxed.

3. a. ( ) It's easy to have a nervous breakdown.

   b. ( ) He is probably working too hard.

   c. ( ) He would like to have a nervous breakdown.

4. a. ( ) He reads slowly.

   b. ( ) He reads quickly.

   c. ( ) When he reads the paper, he reads for the main idea only.

5. a. ( ) The typewriter is broken.

   b. ( ) You didn't turn on the typewriter.

   c. ( ) The plug isn't in the socket.

6. a. ( ) He dates a lot of girls.

   b. ( ) He plays with the boys seven nights a week.

   c. ( ) Girls invite him out every night.

7. a. ( ) Come anytime this weekend.

   b. ( ) Please make an appointment before you come.

   c. ( ) You should buy something this weekend.

8. a. ( ) The secretary took him to see the city.

   b. ( ) The secretary took him on a tour of the company.

   c. ( ) The first day he worked for the president's secretary.

9. a. ( ) She couldn't sleep.

   b. ( ) She wanted to finish the book.

   c. ( ) She is tired of the novel.

10. a. ( ) She is probably looking for a job.

    b. ( ) She covers her face with the newspaper.

    c. ( ) She is very involved in her job.

11.   a. ( )   You didn't put water in the kettle.

      b. ( )   There is no gas.

      c. ( )   There was no flame under the kettle.

12.   a. ( )   She is a show-off.

      b. ( )   She talks like Marilyn Monroe.

      c. ( )   She acted like Marilyn Monroe on TV.

13.   a. ( )   Don't forget to wash the clothes.

      b. ( )   Turn on the dishwasher.

      c. ( )   Exchange the washing machine this afternoon.

V. FILL IN

DIRECTIONS: Fill in the blanks with the correct preposition or particle. (Note: Number 13 requires an adverb.)

Dear Paul,

My first two days in America have been fun. Yesterday, I dropped

_____ your cousin's house. She was so nice that I took her
    1

_____ for dinner.
    2

We stayed _____ all night speaking English. In the morning,
    3

she showed me _____ the city. Don't worry, I didn't bury
    4

myself _____ my guidebook.
    5

When I got home after the tour, I put my feet _____ and
    6

skimmed _____ some magazines.
    7

Tonight I am having some friends _____ for dinner. I guess
    8

I'll plug _____ the stereo and switch _____ the music.
    9   10

Then I'll turn _____ the stove and put the TV dinners in the
                    11

oven. I'll probably liven _____ the meal with some wine and
                                  12

take it _____ the rest of the night.
              13

Sincerely yours,

Eugene

PRACTICAL APPLICATION

Pedro is going to California for a working vacation. He made a list of things to do. Read the list and then make up sentences using the idioms in parentheses.

People to contact: Jim Vincent (805) 573-2190
                       Peggy de Benedictis (213) 903-1517
Buy a guidebook and a road map
Invite some business associates for dinner
Borrow a guitar for the party
Rent a car to go to the beach on the weekend

1. (drop by) _____

_____

2. (take out) _____

_____

3. (skim through) _____

_____

4. (show around) _____

_____

5. (have over) _____

_____

6. (liven up) _____

_____

7. (take it easy) _____

_____

ADDITIONAL EXERCISES

1. Make up a story about the picture at the beginning of the chapter. Use as many idioms as possible. This exercise can be written or oral.
2. Ask each other questions about the picture. You must use an idiom in your response.
3. Use the lines below the picture for a dictation exercise. The teacher or a student dictates the introductory passage and the students write it.
4. Rewrite the introductory passage in the future tense (use *will* and *going to*). Write the passage in the third person singular (he).

IMMIGRATION

Immigration

INTRODUCTORY PASSAGE

Alexander Kaletski was an actor, painter, and songwriter in the Soviet Union. He **had** fame, money, an apartment in the center of Moscow, and **the right to** perform abroad. But in 1975 he **emigrated from** Russia. It was impossible for him to **live under** the repressive Soviet regime. He loved freedom and wrote many songs about it. But he was **prohibited from** singing these songs in the open. So he had to have underground concerts.

> *I sang to my friends for ten years,*
> *In attics and cellars we shed tears;*
> *We dreamed of freedom long ago.*
> *The time has come to sing to the foe!*

The secret police began to **spy on** him. For singing songs which were **against** the government, he could have been **exiled to** Siberia.

> *Smell of corpses, odor of charring flesh—*
> *Curl more joyfully, smoke of our land!*
> *Ah you, Mother, Mother Russia,*
> *Crematorium of human destiny.*

Alexander could have been arrested any day. He had only one choice—to leave the country. He knew that if he **defected from** the Soviet Union, he would be **cut off from** his family forever. So he **went through the proper channels** and **applied for** a visa. He **looked forward to** immigrating to the U.S.

For seven months he was **kept in suspense**, but finally he got permission to leave. He had to **part with** almost everything. He took only a guitar, and his songs which he **smuggled out** in the cuffs of his pants.

143

Goodbye, Russia
Farewell golden cupolas,
*I am **leaving for** America*
To discover my love for Russia.

P.S. Alexander Kaletski is the illustrator for this book.

NOTES

IDIOMS AND THE POSITION OF THEIR OBJECTS	*GRAMMATICAL NOTES*	*STYLE*
1. have [the right] to [ ]		
2. emigrate from [ ]	object is usually a noun	
3. live under [ ]	object is usually a noun	
4. prohibit [ ] from [ ]	usually passive object of the prep. is -*ing* form	formal
5. spy on [ ]		
6. be against [ ]		
7. exile [ ] to [ ]	usually passive object of the prep. is usually a noun	

8.   defect from   [   ] _____ object is usually a noun _____

_____

9.   cut   [   ]   off from   [   ] usually passive ____

_____

10.   go through   [the proper channels]   _____

_____

11.   apply for   [   ]   _____

_____

12.   look forward to   [   ] _____ often followed by -*ing* form _____

_____

13.   immigrate to   [   ]   _____ object is usually a noun _____

_____

14.   keep   [   ]   in   [suspense] often passive _____

_____

15.   part with   [   ]   _____

_____

16.   smuggle   [   ]   out   _____

_____

17.   leave for   [   ]   _____ object is usually a noun _____

_____

Use this page for one or more of the following exercises:

- Write the meaning of the idiom.
- Write sample sentences.
- Look for the idioms in short stories, novels, newspapers, or magazines, and copy the sentences containing them.
- Give examples of appropriate direct objects or objects of the preposition for each idiom that requires an object.
- Practice saying the idioms with correct stress. In general, verbs and particles are stressed, but prepositions are unstressed.

I. DEFINITIONS

DIRECTIONS: Mark the answer that is the closest synonym for the italicized idioms.

1. He *has the right to* contact his lawyer.

    a. ( ) must
    b. ( ) is entitled to
    c. ( ) sends letters to

2. They *emigrated from* Germany.

    a. ( ) moved to
    b. ( ) were born in
    c. ( ) left their own country to live in another

3. We can't *live under* a dictatorship.

    a. ( ) exist under the rule of
    b. ( ) enjoy
    c. ( ) travel to

4. You are *prohibited from* smoking on elevators.

    a. ( ) trying not to
    b. ( ) asked not to
    c. ( ) forbidden to

5. An FBI agent has been *spying on* that revolutionary group.

        a. ( ) secretly watching
        b. ( ) reporting information to
        c. ( ) trying to kill

6. Speaking to reporters *is against* the president's wishes.

        a. ( ) is contary to
        b. ( ) is in agreement with
        c. ( ) goes with

7. He was *exiled to* a small island near Greece.

        a. ( ) invited to
        b. ( ) transferred to
        c. ( ) sent away to (as punishment)

8. While the Russian ballet dancer Nureyev was on tour in Paris, he *defected from* the Soviet Union.

        a. ( ) missed
        b. ( ) spoke about
        c. ( ) changed his allegiance from one country to another

9. When he was hospitalized, he was *cut off from* his friends and family.

        a. ( ) angry with
        b. ( ) restricted from having contact with
        c. ( ) visited by

10. If you want to get a student visa, you must *go through the proper channels.*

        a. ( ) do something the prescribed way
        b. ( ) get a lot of information
        c. ( ) be patient

11. She *applied for* a driver's license.

        a. ( ) practiced for
        b. ( ) needed
        c. ( ) requested in writing

12. Her father isn't *looking forward to* his retirement.

        a. ( ) thinking about with pleasure
        b. ( ) planning
        c. ( ) concerned about

13. The whole family wants to *immigrate to* the United States.

        a. ( ) move to a new country
        b. ( ) leave
        c. ( ) find work in

14. After applying for the job, he was *kept in suspense* for two weeks.

        a. ( ) waiting patiently
        b. ( ) unemployed
        c. ( ) left waiting nervously

15. He was so stingy, he wouldn't *part with* a cent.

        a. ( ) relinquish
        b. ( ) lose
        c. ( ) count

16. He was arrested at the border for trying to *smuggle* a national treasure *out* of the country.

        a. ( ) buy outside
        b. ( ) sell outside
        c. ( ) take out illegally

17. We are *leaving for* Las Vegas tomorrow.

        a. ( ) traveling to
        b. ( ) going away from
        c. ( ) immigrating to

II. WORD ASSOCIATION

DIRECTIONS: Two of the three choices below can be used with the idiom. Mark the *two* answers that can be used to complete each sentence correctly.

1. The young manager applied for _____.

        a. ( ) a raise
        b. ( ) the position
        c. ( ) the vice-president

2. The sailor defected from _____.

        a. ( ) Poland
        b. ( ) the navy school
        c. ( ) the other side

3. Your _____ didn't go through the proper channels.

        a. ( ) telephone
        b. ( ) application
        c. ( ) complaint

4. It's a tragedy to be cut off from _____.

        a. ( ) your family
        b. ( ) your finger
        c. ( ) your friends

5. When are you leaving for _____?

        a. ( ) the music
        b. ( ) home
        c. ( ) Germany

6. They are looking forward to _____.

        a. ( ) their trip around the world
        b. ( ) getting sick
        c. ( ) returning home

7. She was arrested for smuggling _____ out of the country.

        a. ( ) drugs
        b. ( ) gold coins
        c. ( ) underwear

8. He immigrated to _____.

        a. ( ) Texas
        b. ( ) Australia
        c. ( ) this country

9. Her husband won't part with _____.

        a. ( ) a cent
        b. ( ) their Saint Bernard
        c. ( ) the loan

10. _____ kept us in suspense until the last minute.

        a. ( ) The movie
        b. ( ) The consulate
        c. ( ) The job

11. You are prohibited from _____.

        a. ( ) the school
        b. ( ) smoking in this section of the theatre
        c. ( ) walking on the grass

12. He was exiled to _____.

        a. ( ) a tiny island
        b. ( ) his mother land
        c. ( ) a small village

13. Each person has the right to _____.

        a. ( ) say what he wants
        b. ( ) get a job
        c. ( ) employ

14. They hated living under _____.

        a. ( )   an emperor
        b. ( )   the citizens
        c. ( )   a dictator

15. Organizing strikes is against _____.

        a. ( )   company policy
        b. ( )   the law in some countries
        c. ( )   your boss

16. She emigrated from _____.

        a. ( )   Colombia
        b. ( )   Mars
        c. ( )   a small country in Asia

17. The agent spied on _____.

        a. ( )   the immigrants
        b. ( )   a colleague
        c. ( )   himself

THE POSITION OF THE OBJECT

DIRECTIONS: Fill in *one* of the blanks (a or b) in each sentence with the object given in parentheses. Each sentence requires an object.

1. They are spying _____ on _____. (her)
                      a   b

2. He wasn't totally _____ against _____. (it)
                      a   b

3. We couldn't live _____ under _____. (that system)
                      a   b

4. The former king was exiled _____ to _____. (a tiny island)
                      a   b

5. He plans to defect _____ from _____. (his
    a   b
    country)

6. For many years, she was cut off_____from _____.
    a   b
    (him)

7. We are leaving _____for _____. (London)
    a   b

8. He didn't smuggle _____ out _____. (it)
    a   b

9. She emigrated _____ from _____. (Bulgaria)
    a   b

10. We didn't want to part _____ with _____. (it)
    a   b

11. She kept _____ in _____ suspense. (him)
    a   b

12. He wants to immigrate _____ to _____. (this
    a   b
    country)

13. We're looking forward _____ to _____. (it)
    a   b

14. They were prohibited _____ from _____.
    a   b
    (smoking)

15. He never applied _____ for _____. (it)
    a   b

16. You must go _____ through _____. (the proper
    a   b
    channels)

17. You have the right _____ to _____. (it)
    a   b

IV. LISTENING COMPREHENSION ANSWER SHEET

DIRECTIONS: You will hear a short dialogue followed by a question. After you hear each question, read the three choices and mark the response that answers the question correctly.

1. a. ( ) The United States
   b. ( ) Poland
   c. ( ) Argentina

2. a. ( ) No, there is nothing she can do.
   b. ( ) Yes, she can appeal.
   c. ( ) It isn't necessary because she can stay here and finish her education.

3. a. ( ) No, because it will be hard for him.
   b. ( ) Yes, although he knows it will be hard in the beginning.
   c. ( ) No, because he doesn't like the Middle East.

4. a. ( ) He is going to apply for permanent resident status in one week.
   b. ( ) He just got an answer.
   c. ( ) He is still waiting for an answer.

5. a. ( ) A military dictatorship.
   b. ( ) A communist country.
   c. ( ) A democracy.

6. a. ( ) His wife is a spy.
   b. ( ) His wife has another man.
   c. ( ) His wife likes to smoke.

7. a. ( ) He left his country and then tried to go back.
   b. ( ) He was a spy in the Soviet Union.
   c. ( ) He wouldn't leave the Soviet Union.

8. a. ( ) The woman wanted to keep everything.
   b. ( ) The woman's husband wanted to keep everything.
   c. ( ) They had enough suitcases to carry everything.

9. a. ( ) In their homeland.
   b. ( ) In Canada.
   c. ( ) On a trip.

10.   a.   ( )   Antiques and jewelry.

      b.   ( )   Handicrafts.

      c.   ( )   Antiques, jewelry, and handicrafts.

11.   a.   ( )   Nobody wants to offer the man a job.

      b.   ( )   The man is a permanent resident.

      c.   ( )   The man can't work because of his visa.

12.   a.   ( )   In the west.

      b.   ( )   In Siberia.

      c.   ( )   In Moscow.

13.   a.   ( )   He became the best salesman.

      b.   ( )   He was fired.

      c.   ( )   He didn't sign the petition and was fired.

14.   a.   ( )   He defected.

      b.   ( )   He immigrated to the Soviet Union.

      c.   ( )   He was forced out by his government.

15.   a.   ( )   Because he wants to go home.

      b.   ( )   He probably didn't take the necessary steps to stay.

      c.   ( )   He got an extension of stay.

V. FILL IN

DIRECTIONS: Fill in the blanks with the correct preposition or particle.

Alexander Kaletski had fame, money, an apartment in the center

of Moscow, and the right _____ perform abroad. But in 1975 he
                              1

emigrated _____ Russia. He could not live _____ the re-
                 2   3

pressive Soviet regime which prohibited him _____ singing his
                                                      4

songs about freedom.

He continued to sing, underground, and the secret police began to spy＿＿＿＿＿ him. It was illegal to sing songs which were＿＿＿＿＿
₅   ₆

the government. He could have been exiled＿＿＿＿＿ Siberia for
₇

such songs. Eventually, he had only one choice—to leave the country.

He thought about defecting＿＿＿＿＿ the Soviet Union, but he knew
₈

he would be cut＿＿＿＿＿from his family forever. So he went
₉

＿＿＿＿＿ the proper channels and applied＿＿＿＿＿ a visa. He
₁₀   ₁₁

looked＿＿＿＿＿ to immigrating＿＿＿＿＿ the U.S.
₁₂   ₁₃

The government kept him＿＿＿＿＿ suspense for seven months
₁₄

but finally gave him permission to leave. He had to part＿＿＿＿＿
₁₅

almost everything. When he left＿＿＿＿＿America, he took only a
₁₆

guitar, and his songs which he smuggled＿＿＿＿＿ in the cuffs of his
₁₇

pants.

VI. ADDITIONAL EXERCISES

1. Make up a story about the picture at the beginning of the chapter. Use as many idioms as possible. This exercise can be written or oral.
2. Ask each other questions about the picture. You must use an idiom in your response.
3. Use the lines below the picture for a dictation exericse. The teacher or a student dictates the introductory passage and the students write it.
4. Rewrite the introductory passage by changing each sentence to a question. Keep the same verb tense.

GENERAL REVIEW

I. MIXED THEMES

Sunday in the Park

DIRECTIONS: Look at the chapter opening drawing. Then, next to each idiom below, write a sentence describing the picture. Remember to use the idiom in your sentence.

1. (coop up in) _____

_____

2. (pick on) _____

_____

3. (drive out of one's mind) _____

_____

4. (put up with) _____

_____

5. (put on) _____

_____

6. (pull on) _____

_____

7. (head for) _____

_____

8. (stop off) _____

_____

158

9. (get to) _____

_____

10. (take it easy) _____ _____

_____

II. CONTRASTING IDIOMS

DIRECTIONS: Mark the letter of the response which correctly completes each sentence below.

1. He came _____ an interesting article about the People's Republic of China in the paper.

    a. ( ) in
    b. ( ) across

2. The manager came _____ a good way to save money.

    a. ( ) up with
    b. ( ) out

3. Her job as a saleslady brought her _____ a lot of people.

    a. ( ) into contact with
    b. ( ) to trial

4. He did only four out of seven assignments for the class but he didn't get _____ it. He got a C− in the course.

    a. ( ) rid of
    b. ( ) away with

5. I want to see you. Let's get _____ soon.

    a. ( ) to
    b. ( ) together

159

6. They have a great relationship. They get _____ each other very well.

    a. ( ) along with
    b. ( ) down to business

7. That television show gets _____.

    a. ( ) on my nerves
    b. ( ) out of bed on the wrong side

8. That poem isn't popular because the poet didn't get the idea _____.

    a. ( ) across
    b. ( ) into

9. Platform shoes went _____.

    a. ( ) out of fashion
    b. ( ) through the proper channels

10. He saw her only once and already he has _____ her.

    a. ( ) the right to
    b. ( ) a crush on

11. They are going to live _____.

    a. ( ) together
    b. ( ) under

12. We are taking a vacation in two weeks and we are really looking _____ it.

    a. ( ) forward to
    b. ( ) out on

13. The thief made _____ the jewels before the police arrived.

    a. ( ) a deal with
    b. ( ) off with

14. The doctor made _____ one of the nurses.

                                            a. ( ) a pass at
                                            b. ( ) a living by

15. Our building is going to be completely renovated so we have to move _____ soon and find a new apartment.

                                            a. ( ) out
                                            b. ( ) in

16. He is very sensitive. Please don't pick _____ him.

                                            a. ( ) up
                                            b. ( ) on

17. It's illegal to stop for hitchhikers so you had better just pass him _____.

                                            a. ( ) up
                                            b. ( ) by

18. He spent a week in Chicago trying to sell his new gadget but it didn't pay _____.

                                            a. ( ) off
                                            b. ( ) for

19. That policeman wants you to pull _____.

                                            a. ( ) over
                                            b. ( ) on

20. She got in the car and pulled _____ the parking space in a hurry.

                                            a. ( ) into
                                            b. ( ) out of

21. When he discovered that he was the best salesman in the company, he put _____ a raise.

                                            a. ( ) the blame on
                                            b. ( ) in for

22.   Nobody would put _____ a broken elevator all summer.

      a. ( ) together
      b. ( ) up with

23.   When his alarm clock rang, he got up and put _____ quickly.

      a. ( ) his clothes on
      b. ( ) his feet up

24.   The executive director showed _____ a T-shirt.

      a. ( ) around
      b. ( ) up in

25.   The board of directors won't stand _____ a two-week delay.

      a. ( ) for
      b. ( ) to reason

26.   You're walking much too fast. Please take it _____.

      a. ( ) off
      b. ( ) easy

27.   When he saw Sofia Loren, he couldn't take _____.

      a. ( ) her out
      b. ( ) his eyes off her

28.   To tell you _____ the accident, I need all day.

      a. ( ) about
      b. ( ) the truth

29.   During my road test, I had to turn _____.

      a. ( ) on
      b. ( ) around

30.   Oh come _____! I don't believe you're so famous.

   a.   ( )   in
   b.   ( )   on

31.   While he was in the army, he was cut _____ his new bride.

   a.   ( )   out
   b.   ( )   off from

32.   I'm sorry for interrupting. Please go _____.

   a.   ( )   ahead
   b.   ( )   back to

33.   That plastic necklace doesn't go _____ your silk dress.

   a.   ( )   out of fashion
   b.   ( )   with

34.   They both knew they didn't love each other anymore and finally they had it _____.

   a.   ( )   out
   b.   ( )   over

35.   Her parents are afraid that suave Frenchman has _____ their teenage daughter.

   a.   ( )   designs on
   b.   ( )   an affair with

36.   Some American grandparents will not look _____ their grandchildren for free.

   a.   ( )   out on
   b.   ( )   after

37. The famous actress didn't want the part in the movie because she had to make _____ someone on camera.

    a. ( )   love with
    b. ( )   good time

38. If you take the highway you should make _____.

    a. ( )   good time
    b. ( )   up

39. The furniture in the dollhouse was made _____ chips of wood and scraps of material.

    a. ( )   out of
    b. ( )   off with

40. You have nothing to worry about; the killer is _____.

    a. ( )   behind bars
    b. ( )   fed up

41. The young man was _____ his pretty tutor.

    a. ( )   infatuated with
    b. ( )   against

42. Jogging was _____ for quite a long time.

    a. ( )   in vogue
    b. ( )   up to date

III. THEME ASSOCIATION

DIRECTIONS: Next to each idiom, mark the category it is generally associated with.

1. own up to   ( ) residence   ( ) crime
2. tie up   ( ) crime   ( ) fashion
3. make a pass at   ( ) love   ( ) travel

4.	propose to	( ) work	( ) love
5.	strike up	( ) conversation	( ) crime
6.	back up	( ) fashion	( ) travel
7.	move in	( ) travel	( ) residence
8.	make good time	( ) travel	( ) take it easy
9.	have an affair with	( ) work	( ) love
10.	look out on	( ) crime	( ) residence
11.	make up	( ) fashion	( ) conversation
12.	go through the proper channels	( ) immigration	( ) travel
13.	get it across	( ) conversation	( ) travel
14.	round off	( ) fashion	( ) work
15.	enter into	( ) work	( ) travel
16.	have designs on	( ) love	( ) fashion
17.	get away with	( ) crime	( ) travel
18.	have a crush on	( ) crime	( ) love
19.	wind around one's little finger	( ) fashion	( ) love
20.	drive out of one's mind	( ) travel	( ) anger

IV. WRITE A COMMENT

DIRECTIONS: Write a comment about each of the following sentences using the idioms in parentheses.

I. Review of expressions with in.

1. The apartment will be empty at the end of the month.

   (Example) We're going to move in March 1st. _____ (move in)

   _____

2. She won a million dollars in the lottery.

   _____

   _____ (invest in)

3. Why don't you put that miniskirt in the garbage. Nobody is wearing such short clothes now.

_____

_____ (come in)

4. He had a nervous breakdown.

_____

_____ (hold in)

5. A few months ago they bought a $100,000 house and his wife just had triplets. How will he be able to pay all the bills?

_____

_____ (put in for)

II. *Review of expressions with* on.

6. It's awfully dark in here!

_____

_____ (switch on)

7. The kitchen faces a courtyard.

_____

_____ (look out on)

8. If you ask me, Michael talks too much.

_____

_____ (gets on one's nerves)

9. He saw the same man walking behind him yesterday and today.

_____

_____ (spy on)

10. The football game starts in five minutes and you are not even dressed!

_____

_____ (pull on)

III. *Review of expressions with* out.

11. One partner is rich, but the other doesn't have five cents.

_____

_____ (buy out)

12. Every season he buys the latest suit.

_____

_____ (go out of fashion)

13. Didn't you have *two* roommates?

_____

_____ (move out)

14. One boy gave another a black eye in class today.

_____

_____ (throw out)

15. What are you going to do with all those pieces of material?

_____

_____ (make out of)

IV. Review of expressions with to.

16.   What do you think the decision of the jury will be?

_____

_____ (sentence to)

17.   They have been dating since high school.

_____

_____ (propose to)

18.   He loves to say that everything is better in his country.

_____   _____

_____ (go back to)

19.   These statistics represent the years 1975 to 1978.

_____

_____ (be up to date)

20.   After I bought the car, I discovered it needed a new engine and four new tires.

_____

_____ (to tell you the truth)

V. Review of expressions with up.

21.   My favorite movie was on The Late Show last night.

_____

_____ (stay up)

22. The party is at the best hotel in town.

_____

_____ (dress up)

23. He hates to go to his mother-in-law's house for the holidays.

_____

_____ (make up)

24. It is difficult for her to talk to strangers.

_____

_____ (clam up)

25. It is hard to believe he started his business with a hot dog stand.

_____

_____ (build up)

VI. *Review of expressions with* with.

26. Before moving, you have to decide what you are not going to keep.

_____

_____ (part with)

27. The two superpowers didn't sign the treaty because of one small point.

_____

_____ (disagree with)

28. He couldn't understand why he was being arrested. He was carrying a gun but he hadn't used it.

_____

_____ (charge with)

29. Can you imagine, her father died and two weeks later her mother died!

_____

_____ (cope with)

30. If I were you I would buy this tie to wear with the suit.

_____

_____ (go with)

WRITE A SENTENCE

UNFURNISHED APARTMENTS

2001 5th Ave. 2 Bedrooms—only $570! Modern High-rise. Meet nice people. View of Central Park. Many closets. No pets. A handyman's delight! Make appointment after August 19. Available Sept. 1. Two-year lease. Better Realty, 19 E. 71 St., 5th Fl. 535-0008

DIRECTIONS: Read the advertisement above and then write one sentence next to each idiom below. Remember to use the idiom in your sentence.

1. (skim through) _____

_____

2.   (look out on) _____

_____

3.   (tower over) _____

_____

4.   (bring into contact with) _____

_____

5.   (clutter up) _____

_____

6.   (prohibit from) _____

_____

7.   (fix up) _____

_____

8.   (apply for) _____

_____

9.   (move in) _____

_____

10.   (furnish with) _____

_____

VI. A CROSSWORD PUZZLE OF IDIOMS

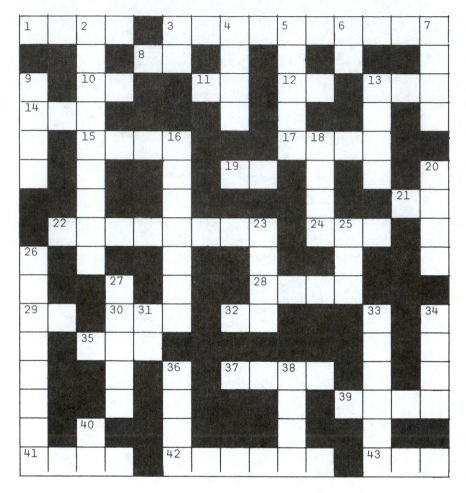

CLUES

ACROSS

1 To drive in reverse = to
   _____ up.

3 He is _____ with a pretty
   girl in his class.

8 Don't put the blame _____
   me!

10 She suddenly came _____
   with a brilliant idea.

DOWN

2 There is no room in this apartment
   it's so _____ up with junk.

3 Somebody broke _____ last
   night and stole everything.

4 In prison he was cut off
   _____ the outside world.

5 By the time the case was brought
   to _____, nobody was
   interested.

11 It's a pleasure to _____ business with you.

12 _____ stands to reason she is angry.

13 They were caught smuggling heroin _____ of the country.

14 Her singing is driving me _____ of my mind.

15 He has to _____ down the purple walls.

17 We went to the restaurant because we didn't feel _____ cooking.

19 To match = to _____ with.

21 This equipment will not _____ up to date very long.

22 That dancer_____ from his country while he was on tour.

24 The robbers made _____ with $2,000,000.

28 Last night we had some friends _____ for dinner.

29 It looks like he is making a pass _____ you.

30 This chair is broken. Why don't you get _____ of it.

32 To establish, to organize = to set _____.

35 The little girl cried when her puppy was _____ over.

37 He is so stingy he won't part _____ a cent.

39 Who can _____ under a repressive regime?

41 If you _____ up in jeans, you won't get the job.

42 Prisoners are _____ up in cells.

43 The police think he will _____ down another victim.

6 The house was valued _____ half a million dollars.

7 This office copier is certainly up to _____!

9 _____ up your sleeves if you don't want to get dirty.

13 Don't lose any sleep _____ the travelers' checks.

16 They were _____ from the building because they never paid the rent.

18 To convince = to talk _____.

20 She _____ in love with a rich man.

23 To visit informally = to _____ by.

25 Where are you heading _____ after the game?

26 His application was denied because he didn't go through the proper _____.

27 She has a _____ on her gym teacher.

31 Is the typewriter plugged _____?

33 He makes a _____ by renovating old buildings.

34 Nobody believed the excuse she _____ up.

36 You must look before you _____ out of a parking space.

38 We made good _____ because there was no traffic.

40 He immigrated _____ the United States.

Appendix A
List of Prepositions
and Particles

PREPOSITIONS	PARTICLES
about	about
across	across
after	after
against	—
—	ahead
along	along
around	around
at	—
—	away
—	back
behind	behind
by	by
down	down
for	—
from	—
in	in
into	—
like	—
of	—
off	off
on	on
out of	out
over	over
through	through
to	to
—	together
under	under
up	up
with	—

Appendix B
Idioms Listed According to Prepositions and Particles

about
complain about
tell about
(not) think twice about

across
come across
cut across
get across

after
look after

against
be against

ahead
go ahead

along
get along with

around
prowl around
show around
turn around
wind somebody around one's little
    finger

at
make a pass at
value at

away
get away with

back
go back to

behind
be behind bars

by
drop by
make a living by
pass by

down
calm down
get down to business
gun down
tone down

for
apply for
arrange for
head for
leave for
pay for
put in for
stand for

from
cut off from
defect from
emigrate from
escape from
evict from
gather from
prohibit from

in
be in vogue
break in
bury oneself in
cash in on
come in
confide in

175

coop up in
fall in love with
hold in
invest in
keep in suspense
move in
plug in
put in for
show up in

into
bring into contact with
enter into
get into
pull into
talk into

like
feel like

of
accuse of
convict of
drive somebody out of his mind
get out of bed on the wrong side
get rid of
go out of fashion
make out of
pull out of

off
cut off from
make off with
pay off
round off
seal off
stop off
sweep somebody off his feet
take off
(can't) take one's eyes off

on
cash in on
come on
get on somebody's nerves
get out of bed on the wrong side
have a crush on

have designs on
look out on
pick on
pull on
put on
put the blame on
spy on
switch on
touch on
turn on

out
branch out
buy out
come out
cut out
drive somebody out of his mind
get out of bed on the wrong side
go out of fashion
have it out
look out on
make out of
move out
pull out of
smuggle out
start out
take out
throw out

over
have over
(not) lose any sleep over
pull over
run over
sign over
tower over

through
go through the proper channels
skim through

to
be up to date
bring to trial
confess to
exile to

get down to business
get to
go back to
have the right to
immigrate to
listen to
look forward to
object to
own up to
propose to
sentence to
(it) stands to reason
to tell you the truth

together
get together
live together
put together

under
live under

up
back up
be fed up
be up to date
build up
clam up
clutter up
come up with
coop up in
dress up
fill up
fix up
keep up with the times
liven up
lock up
make up
own up to
pass up
pick up

put one's feet up
put up with
roll up
set up
show up in
stay up
strike up
tie up
zip up

with
be infatuated with
bring into contact with
charge with
come up with
cope with
deal with
disagree with
do business with
flirt with
furnish with
get along with
get away with
go with
have an affair with
keep up with the times
make a deal with
make love with
make off with
part with
put up with

Miscellaneous (without prepositions or particles)

make good time
take it easy

Appendix C
Idioms Listed Alphabetically

have the right to,	143	put on,	85
head for,	115	put one's feet up,	129
hold in,	100	put the blame on,	53
immigrate to,	143	put together,	85
invest in,	19	put up with,	100
keep in suspense,	143	roll up,	85
keep up with the times,	85	round off,	19
leave for,	144	run over,	115
listen to,	3	seal off,	38
live together,	72	sentence to,	53
live under,	143	set up,	19
liven up,	129	show around,	129
lock up,	53	show up in,	85
look after,	71	sign over,	19
look forward to,	143	skim through,	129
look out on,	38	smuggle out,	143
(not) lose any sleep over,	100	spy on,	143
make a deal with,	19	stand for,	100
make a living by,	20	(it) stands to reason,	3
make a pass at,	71	start out,	115
make good time,	115	stay up,	129
make love with,	72	stop off,	115
make off with,	53	strike up,	3
make out of,	85	sweep somebody off his feet,	72
make up,	3	switch on,	129
move in,	38	take it easy,	129
move out,	38	take off,	85
object to,	100	(can't) take one's eyes off,	71
own up to,	53	take out,	129
part with,	143	talk into,	3
pass by,	115	tell about,	3
pass up,	38	(to) tell you the truth,	3
pay for,	53	(not) think twice about,	100
pay off,	19	throw out,	72
pick on,	100	tie up,	53
pick up,	53	tone down,	38
plug in,	129	touch on,	3
prohibit from,	143	tower over,	38
propose to,	72	turn around,	115
prowl around,	53	turn on,	129
pull into,	115	value at,	19
pull on,	85	wind somebody around one's little	
pull out of,	115	finger,	71
pull over,	115	zip up,	85
put in for,	20		

Appendix D
The Position
of Pronoun
and Noun Objects

CHAPTER 1. Conversation

THE POSITION OF PRONOUN OBJECTS AND NOUN OBJECTS
(The idiom is listed alone if it does not have an object.)

1. **strike up**
   strike up a conversation

2. **gather from**
   gather from your expression

3. **to tell you the truth**

4. **tell about**
   tell her about it
   tell Nancy about your vacation

5. **go ahead**

6. **listen to**
   listen to this
   listen to this story

7. **come on**

8. **make up**
   make it up
   make an excuse up   or   make up an excuse

9. **get across**
   get it across
   get a point across

10. **clam up**

11. **touch on**
    touch on it
    touch on his childhood

12. **it stands to reason**

180

13. **disagree with**
    disagree with him
    disagree with Charles

14. **talk into**
    talk them into it
    talk the couple into buying a new car

CHAPTER 2. *Work*

THE POSITION OF PRONOUN OBJECTS AND NOUN OBJECTS
(The idiom is listed alone if it does not have an object.)

1. **make a deal with**
   make a deal with them
   make a deal with another company

2. **cash in on**
   cash in on it
   cash in on the need for fast food

3. **buy out**
   buy her out
   buy his sister out   or   buy out his sister

4. **sign over**
   sign it over
   sign the property over   or   sign over the property

5. **build up**
   build it up
   build the company up   or   build up the company

6. **set up**
   set it up
   set the institute up   or   set up the institute

7. **branch out**

8. **value at**
   value it at one million
   value the diamond at one million

9. **round off**
   round it off
   round the number off   or   round off the number

10. **bring into contact with**
    bring her into contact with them
    bring Elizabeth into contact with many doctors

11. **arrange for**
    arrange for it
    arrange for a business meeting

12. **do business with**
    do business with them
    do business with Smith and Co.

13. **pay off**

14. **get down to business**

15. **enter into**
    enter into it
    enter into a deal

16. **invest in**
    invest in it
    invest in land

17. **make a living by**
    make a living by singing

18. **deal with**
    deal with them
    deal with all types of people

19. **put in for**
    put in for it
    put in for a raise

CHAPTER 3. *Residence*

THE POSITION OF PRONOUN OBJECTS AND NOUN OBJECTS
(The idiom is listed alone if it does not have an object.)

1. **come across**
   come across it
   come across a photograph

2. **pass up**
   pass it up
   pass a good chance up   or   pass up a good chance

3. **coop up in**
   coop him up in there
   coop the dog up in the closet

4. **tower over**
   tower over us
   tower over our building

5. **be up to date**

6. **look out on**
    look out on a park

7. **clutter up**
    clutter it up
    clutter the room up   or   clutter up the room

8. **tone down**
    tone it down
    tone the color down   or   tone down the color

9. **fix up**
    fix it up
    fix the living room up   or   fix up the living room

10. **move out**

11. **move in**

12. **get rid of**
    get rid of that
    get rid of that ugly couch

13. **furnish with**
    furnish it with antiques
    furnish the apartment with antiques

14. **seal off**
    seal it off
    seal the doorway off   or   seal off the doorway

15. **evict from**
    evict him from here
    evict our neighbor from our building

CHAPTER 4. *Crime*

THE POSITION OF PRONOUN OBJECTS AND NOUN OBJECTS
(The idiom is listed alone if it does not have an object.)

1. **gun down**
    gun them down
    gun the innocent people down   or   gun down the innocent people

2. **break in**

3. **prowl around**
    prowl around there   or   prowl around
    prowl around that neighborhood

4. **tie up**
   tie him up
   tie the pilot up   or   tie up the pilot

5. **make off with**
   make off with them
   make off with the jewels

6. **get away with**
   get away with it
   get away with the crime

7. **pick up**
   pick them up
   pick the murderers up   or   pick up the murderers

8. **lock up**
   lock them up
   lock the criminals up   or   lock up the criminals

9. **bring to trial**
   bring it to trial
   bring the case to trial

10. **own up to**
    own up to it
    own up to the crime

11. **put the blame on**
    put the blame on her
    put the blame on his wife

12. **confess to**
    confess to it
    confess to the murder

13. **accuse of**
    accuse him of it
    accuse the teenager of stealing

14. **charge with**
    charge her with it
    charge the woman with murder

15. **convict of**
    convict him of it
    convict him of forgery

16. **sentence to**
    sentence him to death
    sentence the man to death

17. **be behind bars**

18. **pay for**
     pay for it
     pay for his violence

19. **escape from**
     escape from it
     escape from jail

CHAPTER 5. *Love*

THE POSITION OF PRONOUN OBJECTS AND NOUN OBJECTS
(The idiom is listed alone if it does not have an object.)

1. **look after**
    look after her
    look after the baby

2. **can't take one's eyes off**
    can't take his eyes off her
    can't take his eyes off the girl next to him

3. **flirt with**
    flirt with him
    flirt with a salesman

4. **have a crush on**
    have a crush on him
    have a crush on a singer

5. **have designs on**
    have designs on her
    have designs on his new neighbor

6. **wind around one's little finger**
    wind him around her little finger
    wind the boy around her little finger

7. **get along with**
    get along with her
    get along with his mother-in-law

8. **confide in**
    confide in him
    confide in his brother

9. **sweep off his/her feet**
    sweep her off her feet
    sweep the young girl off her feet

10. **be infatuated with**
    be infatuated with her
    be infatuated with the ballet dancer

11. **have an affair with**
    have an affair with him
    have an affair with her boss

12. **make a pass at**
    make a pass at him
    make a pass at the manager

13. **live together**

14. **propose to**
    propose to her
    propose to his girlfriend

15. **make love with**
    make love with her
    make love with his wife

16. **throw out**
    throw her out
    throw his wife out

17. **fall in love with**
    fall in love with him
    fall in love with a handsome man

18. **get together**

CHAPTER 6. *Fashion*

THE POSITION OF PRONOUN OBJECTS AND NOUN OBJECTS
(The idiom is listed alone if it does not have an object.)

1. **come up with**
   come up with it
   come up with a great idea

2. **make out of**
   make it out of scraps
   make a dress out of scraps

3. **put together**
   put it together
   put the watch together

4. **come out**

5. **come in**

6. **go out of fashion**

7. **put on**
    put it on
    put the jacket on   or   put on the jacket

8. **pull on**
    pull them on
    pull your jeans on   or   pull on your jeans

9. **roll up**
    roll them up
    roll your sleeves up   or   roll up your sleeves

10. **take off**
    take them off
    take your boots off   or   take off your boots

11. **show up in**
    show up in it
    show up in a mink

12. **dress up**

13. **zip up**
    zip it up
    zip my dress up   or   zip up my dress

14. **go with**
    go with that
    go with pants

15. **keep up with the times**

16. **be in vogue**

CHAPTER 7. *Anger*

THE POSITION OF PRONOUN OBJECTS AND NOUN OBJECTS
(The idiom is listed alone if it does not have an object.)

1. **cope with**
    cope with it
    cope with this crisis

2. **drive out of his/her mind**
    drive him out of his mind
    drive her husband out of his mind

3. **get on one's nerves**
    get on her nerves
    get on Mary's nerves

4. **not think twice about**
    not think twice about it
    not think twice about the crime

5. **be fed up**

6. **pick on**
    pick on him
    pick on the little boy

7. **complain about**
    complain about it
    complain about his job

8. **get out of bed on the wrong side**

9. **hold in**
    hold it in
    hold your feelings in   or   hold in your feelings

10. **have out**
    have it out
    have the whole thing out

11. **feel like**
    feel like it
    feel like washing the clothes

12. **put up with**
    put up with it
    put up with all the complaints

13. **stand for**
    stand for it
    stand for his insults

14. **calm down**
    calm her down   or   calm down
    calm the hysterical woman down   or   calm down the hysterical
                                                              woman

15. **not lose any sleep over**
    not lose any sleep over it
    not lose any sleep over the gossip

16. **cut out**
    cut it out
    cut this behavior out   or   cut out this behavior

17. **object to**
     object to it
     object to his rude behavior

CHAPTER 8. *Travel*

THE POSITION OF PRONOUN OBJECTS AND NOUN OBJECTS
(The idiom is listed alone if it does not have an object.)

1. **start out**

2. **back up**
    back it up   **or**   back up
    back the car up   **or**   back up the car

3. **pass by**
    pass by it
    pass by the store

4. **pull into**
    pull into the space

5. **pull out of**
    pull out of the lot

6. **pull over**
    pull it over   **or**   pull over
    pull the car over

7. **get into**
    get into it
    get into the next lane

8. **cut across**
    cut across that field

9. **get to**
    get to it
    get to the opposite side

10. **fill up**
    fill it up
    fill the tank up   **or**   fill up the tank

11. **turn around**
    turn it around   **or**   turn around
    turn the car around

12. **stop off**

13. **go back to**
    go back to the light

14. **head for**
    head for it
    head for the zoo

15. **run over**
    run him over
    run the dog over   or   run over the dog

16. **make good time**

CHAPTER 9. *Take It Easy*

THE POSITION OF PRONOUN OBJECTS AND NOUN OBJECTS
(The idiom is listed alone if it does not have an object.)

1. **take it easy**

2. **liven up**
   liven it up
   liven the party up   or   liven up the party

3. **take out**
   take her out
   take his girlfriend out   or   take out his girlfriend

4. **drop by**

5. **stay up**

6. **skim through**
   skim through it
   skim through the chapter

7. **show around**
   show them around
   show the guests around

8. **put one's feet up**
   put his feet up

9. **have over**
   have him over
   have a friend over

10. **turn on**
    turn it on
    turn the light on   or   turn on the light

11. **switch on**
    switch it on
    switch the radio on   or   switch on the radio

12. **plug in**
     plug it in
     plug the iron in   **or**   plug in the iron
13. **bury oneself in**
     bury yourself in it
     bury yourself in your book

CHAPTER 10. *Immigration*

THE POSITION OF PRONOUN OBJECTS AND NOUN OBJECTS
(The idiom is listed alone if it does not have an object.)

1. **have the right to**
    have the right to it
    have the right to work

2. **emigrate from**
    emigrate from his country

3. **live under**
    live under this system

4. **prohibit from**
    prohibit her from staying
    prohibit the student from staying

5. **spy on**
    spy on him
    spy on the artist

6. **be against**
    be against it
    be against the government

7. **exile to**
    exile him to a remote village
    exile the leader to a remote village

8. **defect from**
    defect from his country

9. **cut off from**
    cut her off from them
    cut the politician off from her group

10. **go through the proper channels**

11. **apply for**
    apply for it
    apply for a visa

12. **look forward to**
    look forward to it
    look forward to the trip

13. **immigrate to**
    immigrate to this country

14. **keep in suspense**
    keep him in suspense
    keep the applicant in suspense

15. **part with**
    part with it
    part with the necklace

16. **smuggle out**
    smuggle it out
    smuggle the antiques out   or   smuggle out the antiques

17. **leave for**
    leave for Paris

Appendix E
Listening Comprehension Transcripts

Conversation

Part I

1. *Man:*   You should never strike up a conversation with a man on the street. Don't you know how dangerous it is!

   Woman: I usually don't, but I couldn't find the restaurant and he looked very respectable.

   ?   Why was the man upset?

2. *Woman:*   Yes, of course I would love to see London, Rome and Athens, but what I really want is to enjoy Paris while I'm in Europe.

   Man: I gather from what you're saying you would prefer to spend more time in one city instead of seeing everything in Europe.

   ?   What did the man understand the woman to say?

3. *Man:*   What did the senator say when the newsman asked him about his romance with the rock singer?

   Woman: I heard he just said, "Come on."

   ?   What did the senator mean?

4. *Woman:*   Did you ever hear your voice on a tape recorder?

   Man: Yes. I was so shocked I couldn't listen to it.

   ?   What did the man probably do when he heard his voice?

5. *Woman:*   Doctor, do you think it is something serious?

   Man: To tell you the truth, I don't know.

   ?   What was the doctor's response to the woman's question?

Part II

1. Arthur didn't want to join the club because the swimming pool was very small and there were only two tennis courts. But in the end, the owner talked him into it.

2. In the interview, the former First Lady discussed her operation, her marriage, and even touched on her addiction to drugs.

3. Caroline thinks she should get a divorce but her mother-in-law disagrees with her.

4. When we asked Anthony where he got his middle name, Winston, he said he wasn't given a middle name at birth so he just made it up.

5. Fifty percent of his income comes from tips but he doesn't want to tell the Internal Revenue Service about it.

6. When the lawyer began to question the victim about the robbery, she tried to answer but suddenly clammed up.

7. The American Kennel Club lists over a hundred breeds of dogs. It stands to reason it would be difficult to decide what kind you want.

8. On most tests if you can't find the answer to a question, it's better to go ahead to the next one than to spend all your time on a difficult one.

9. Paul is the only person I know who would disagree with Benjamin Franklin's saying—"There never was a good war or a bad peace."

10. When the travel agent said you were taking your vacation during the "dog days," he was trying to get across the idea that the weather would be hot and humid in July, August, and early September.

Work

1. When her flight was cancelled because of the snow, the airline arranged for a hotel room for her free of charge.

2. The United States does business with Canada, Japan, West Germany, and the United Kingdom. This includes both import and export.

3. They spent so much time talking about their friends they never got down to business.

4. Andrew Carnegie, the steel industrialist, set up several foundations for education and research.

5. If he doesn't get a new job, he is going to put in for a raise at his present company.

6. Although the auctioneer said the painting was valued at a quarter of a million, it was sold for $100,000.

7. He makes a living by playing tennis.

8. During the Great Depression of 1929, he needed cash so he let his rich partner buy him out.

9. The two countries just entered into a five-year trade agreement.

10. John D. Rockefeller founded the Standard Oil Company. He built up the company to the point that it had almost a total monopoly on the oil industry in the late 1800's.

11. At the beginning of the interview, the Vice President offered me a salary of $17,685; but at the end, he rounded it off to $18,000.

12. Before the old man died he signed over all his possessions to his grandson.

13. Because he worked in the complaint office, he had to deal with angry customers all day.

14. After a two-week strike, the sanitation workers and the management finally made a deal with each other.

15. According to the 1970 census, the population of the U.S. was 203,211,926 which can be rounded off to 203,000,000.

16. He invested all his savings in a clever gadget but it never paid off.

17. Joining the Teamsters Union, the largest labor union in the Unite States, brought him into contact with lots of other truckdrivers.

18. They cashed in on the demand for American-made products n Japan.

19. The U.S. gained its independence from England in 1776. The ew government was set up in 1789 with George Washington as th irst president.

20. The American capitalist, Cornelius Vanderbilt, started the shipping business but then branched out and bought railrc ls.

Residence

1. Denise decided not to take the apartment because it wou cost too much money to fix it up. Why didn't Denise rent the a tment?

2. When she realized the apartment had a southern expo re she got rid of the venetian blinds in order to enjoy the sunlight.

3. They moved out of their apartment on Tuesday but will be staying with relatives for five days because they can't move in to their new co-op until then.

4. Mark's new apartment looks out on 79th Street but the entrance is on Park Avenue.

5. There is always friction between Lois and her roommate Debbie because Lois always clutters up the bathroom with dirty laundry.

6. The apartment is in excellent condition except for the bathroom, but that is no reason to pass up a deal like that.

7. So many people died in the fire because the management had sealed off one of the exits in the movie theatre and the two that were open weren't enough.

8. If the landlord won't tone down the walls, the new tenants are not going to sign the lease.

9. They couldn't see the apartment because the present tenant is being evicted from the building and he won't let anybody in.

10. The secretaries complained to their boss because they were cooped up in a tiny office with no window all day.

11. I was amazed when I came across those ugly billboards in the picturesque village.

12. If they were closer to each other, the World Trade Center would tower over the Empire State Building.

13. My dentist raised his rates because he recently furnished his office with new equipment.

14. That department store lost a lot of customers because its merchandise is not exactly up to date.

15. You are going to lose your deposit on the apartment if you move out before your lease is finished.

Crime

1. The bank robber was sentenced to seven years in prison. After he had been behind bars for twenty-two months, he was released.

2. The Boston Strangler was locked up in 1963 for killing ten women.

3. He was such a cute little boy that he could get away with murder.

4. In Dostoyevsky's novel, *Crime and Punishment,* Raskolnikov murders an old pawnbroker and her sister, and makes off with some jewelry.

5. As soon as she was behind bars she began to think about the best way to escape from jail.

6. The boy committed suicide in his senior year of college and his parents put the blame on the school.

7. She refused to go into her apartment because she thought she heard somebody prowling around.

8. In Muslim countries criminals must pay for their crimes. According to Islamic Law, the punishment for stealing is amputation of the hand.

9. According to the newspaper report, an off-duty policeman was charged with murder.

10. The detectives found the killer because of the knot he always made when he tied up his victims.

11. The killer called "Son of Sam" was picked up after a long search. The police discovered who the murderer was through a parking ticket.

12. When the store detective caught the teenager stealing a Beatles' record, the boy owned up to stealing thirty records the week before.

13. A former Vice President resigned when he was accused of not reporting $29,500 on his income tax report. He was sentenced to three years probation and had to pay a fine of $10,000.

14. As soon as he heard there was an eyewitness, he confessed to the shooting.

15. During one presidential campaign burglars were caught at the Democratic Party's headquarters. They were breaking in.

Love

Part I

1. In Nabokov's novel, *Lolita,* Humbert Humbert couldn't take his eyes off the heroine.
   How did he feel about her?

2. When Lolita's mother discovered Humbert's diary, she realized that Humbert had designs on her daughter.
   What did the diary probably say?

3. When Lolita's mother was killed by a car, Humbert looked after his step daughter.
   What did he do after the girl's mother died?

4. Most of the novel describes Humbert's life with Lolita while they were driving from town to town and living together in various hotels.
   Were Lolita and Humbert husband and wife?

5. After Lolita escaped from Humbert, he searched for her a long time. At the end of the novel they get together in her decrepit house. Her husband and a neighbor are also present.
   What happens at the end of the novel?

Part II

1.   *Woman:* Did you hear about Bill and Nancy?
     Man: Yes, it's unbelievable. They got along with each other for two years but as soon as he proposed to her they began to fight constantly. I think they are going to cancel everything.
     ?   When did Bill and Nancy begin to have problems?

2.   *Woman:* Did you notice that every time Peter sees Margaret in the corridor he makes a pass at her?
     Woman: I wasn't sure, but I thought he was interested in her.
     ?   What did Peter probably do?

3.   *Man:*   How was the cocktail party last night? Did you meet anyone interesting?
     Woman: Yes, I met someone tall, dark, and very handsome and I already have a terrible crush on him.
     ?   What did the woman say about the man she met?

4.   *Man:*   How was your trip to Italy with Mary?
     Woman: Fine, but we didn't have much peace. The Italian men were flirting with us all the time.
     ?   What did the woman say about her trip?

5.   *Man:*   I hear you're falling in love with Joan. Be careful, she can wind any guy around her little finger.
     Man: I know what you mean!
     ?   What did the first man say about Joan?

Fashion

1.   A former First Lady made the American designer Halston famous when she showed up for her husband's inauguration in a Halston pillbox hat.

2.   Short skirts first came in in the 1920's.

3.   During the 1960's, hemlines changed frequently. Minis, midis, and maxis all came out during that period.

4.   If the shoes go with your dress, buy them, even if they cost $110.

5.   She is a buyer for a chain of boutiques so she goes to Paris every year to keep up with the times.

6.   When she took off her sloppy dress and put on that chic outfit in the dressing room, she looked like a new person.

7. That style suit came out last year but it wasn't really in vogue until this year.

8. She can't sew, so when she buys pants that are too long she just rolls them up.

9. All of his ties went out of fashion about fifteen years ago, but he doesn't want to throw them away because he is sure they will be in vogue once again.

10. These shoes feel like they were made out of pieces of metal.

11. American fashion designers are famous for putting together clothes that emphasize casual comfort.

12. When he zipped up the pants, they split at the seams.

13. She likes support pantyhose because she can pull them on in a hurry and they don't run as easily as sheer pantyhose.

14. Everybody dressed up for the birthday party except Peter.

15. The new designer went bankrupt because he didn't come up with any innovative designs. He simply copied the clothes of Yves Saint Laurent and Dior.

Anger

1. *Man:* Why won't you go to the party, honey?
   Woman: I'm not going because I just don't feel like it.
   ? Why won't the woman go to the party?

2. *Woman:* Where are you going at this time of night?
   Man: I'm checking into a hotel. For the past two hours you have been complaining about everything I do.
   ? What was the woman doing before this conversation?

3. *Man:* Did you see Daniel after he was notified that he was fired?
   Woman: Yes, he looked like a madman when he walked out of J.B.'s office, and it took a few hours before he could calm down.
   ? How did Daniel react to the news?

4. *Woman:* I heard there was a scene at the dinner last night.
   Man: You're right. Nobody at the table could put up with Dr. Lawrence. He proposed that life would be much better in this country if we had a segregation policy.
   ? How did the other guests feel about Dr. Lawrence's suggestion?

5. *Woman:* I couldn't believe it when she told the psychiatrist he ought to have his head examined.

   Man: Neither could I. It looked like he wanted to explode but somehow he held in his feelings.

   ? How did the psychiatrist react to what the woman said?

6. *Man:* Why was she screaming?

   Woman: Paul was picking on her and she got angry.

   ? What did Paul probably say to the woman?

7. *Man:* When the Eiffel Tower was built for the Centennial Exposition of 1889, it was the tallest structure in the world—300 meters.

   Woman: That's true, but most Parisians objected to the structure on aesthetic grounds.

   ? How did the Parisians react to the Eiffel Tower?

8. *Woman:* What was your session like?

   Man: The therapist told me to lie down on the couch and talk about whatever I wanted. After that he didn't say anything and this

   ? drove me out of my mind.

   What happened?

9. *Woman:* I heard they didn't sign the contract.

   Man: Yes, it's too bad but I'm certainly not going to lose any sleep over it.

   ? What was the man's reaction?

10. *Woman:* Did Helen tell you about the fight she and her husband had last night?

    Man: Yes, it really got on his nerves when he found that photograph in her pocketbook.

    ? How did Helen's husband react to the photograph?

11. *Man:* Americans don't think twice about using garbage for landfill.

    Woman: Yes, I've heard that part of Manhattan is built on garbage. In my country it would be impossible to even talk about this!

    ? How do Americans feel about using garbage for landfill?

12. *Woman:* Mark is in pretty serious trouble, isn't he?

    Man: Yes, he lost $40,000 in the stock market recently. I thought his wife would be fed up with him but she seems to be able to cope with the whole thing.

    ? How did Mark's wife react to the loss?

13.   *Woman:*   I don't like back-seat drivers and I am not going to stand for your constant warnings.

        Man: Okay, okay. If you want me to cut it out, just ask me nicely.

        ?   What is the man going to do?

14.   *Man:*   You and your husband have been angry at each other for weeks. Why don't you have it out and both of you will feel better.

        Woman: You're probably right, but I'm afraid he won't be able to control himself if we start to discuss it.

        ?   What is the woman worried about?

15.   *Woman:*   Don't talk to the boss today. He must have gotten out of bed on the wrong side.

        Man: No, his arthritis is probably bothering him. It's awfully damp out.

        ?   What is wrong with the boss according to the man?

Travel

1. How do you get to the gas station from the post office?
2. What do you have to do when you pull out of the parking lot behind the post office?
3. If you want to buy something at the drug store but you go past it by mistake, what do you have to do?
4. Where can you fill up the tank?
5. If you are entering the park and you are headed for Route 17, what will you pass by?
6. On the way to the post office, you want to buy a hamburger. What should you do?
7. What do you have to do if you want to get into the park?
8. What will happen if you turn around in front of the church?
9. If you think you have run over a dog, what should you do?
10. If you have to go from the post office to the church and you want to make good time, what is the best thing to do?

Take It Easy

1. She was having friends over at eight, but she was still at the club at 7:50.
2. The morning after his bachelor's party he had a terrible hangover so he just put his feet up and did nothing.

3. If he doesn't take it easy, he will most likely have a nervous breakdown.

4. Instead of skimming through the newspaper, he spends two and a half hours reading it every day.

5. The typewriter doesn't work because it isn't plugged in.

6. What a playboy he is! He takes a different girl out every night of the week.

7. Why don't you drop by this weekend. I'll be home Saturday and Sunday.

8. On his first day of work, he was shown around the factory by the president's secretary.

9. She is tired because she stayed up all night to finish the novel.

10. On the way to work, she buries herself in the help-wanted ads.

11. The water didn't boil because you didn't turn the gas on.

12. Her imitation of Marilyn Monroe livened up the talk-show.

13. Please switch on the washing machine this afternoon.

Immigration

1. *Woman:* You have an unusual accent. Where were you born?
   Man: Well, I was born in Poland, but I spent most of my life in Argentina, and five years ago I immigrated to the U.S.
   ? Where did the man emigrate from five years ago?

2. *Man:* Paul told me your application for a student visa was denied. What are you going to do?
   Woman: I don't know. I have the right to appeal but I think I'll return to my country and finish my education there.
   ? Can the woman do anything about her visa status?

3. *Woman:* How do you feel about moving to the Middle East?
   Man: I'm looking forward to it even though it will be difficult the first year.
   ? Is the man happy about moving to the Middle East?

4. *Woman:* Well, don't keep me in suspense. Did they approve your application for permanent resident status?
   Man: I'm not trying to keep you in suspense; I didn't get an answer yet. It will probably take another week.
   ? What is the man's situation at the present time?

5. *Man:* Look at this paycheck! The government took almost 30% in taxes!

   Woman: Stop complaining. You're lucky to be living in a free country. How would you like to live under a military dictatorship? Then you would really have something to complain about!

   ? What kind of country are these people living in?

6. *Woman:* I don't think Bob and Janet are happy together anymore.

   Man: Yes, I heard that Bob paid someone to spy on Janet after he found a book of matches from the Park Hotel in her purse.

   ? What does Bob probably think about his wife Janet?

7. *Man:* Do you think Michael is a spy?

   Woman: I don't know but I have never heard of anybody emigrating from the Soviet Union and then applying for permission to go back.

   ? Why does the woman think Michael is a spy?

8. *Man:* I have never seen so many suitcases in my life!

   Woman: When we were leaving Tokyo, my husband wouldn't part with anything so we brought everything back with us.

   ? Why did the couple take so many things from Tokyo?

9. *Man:* Why don't you immigrate to Canada instead of coming here on short visits?

   Woman: I would like to but I couldn't live if I were cut off from my family and friends.

   ? Where are the woman's family and friends?

10. *Woman:* I have a lot of things I would like to bring back to the States with me. Do you think I will have any problem at customs?

    Man: Somebody told me you can't take anything but handicrafts out of the country. The only way to take antiques, or jewelry is to smuggle them out, but that's illegal.

    ? According to the man, what can be taken out of the country legally?

11. *Man:* Do you think I can start working tomorrow?

    Woman: There is one small problem, Mr. Rivera. If you were a permanent resident, we could hire you, but since you have a tourist visa, you are prohibited from working in this country.

    ? What is the problem?

12. *Man:*   Sushlov applied for a position in Moscow but when the government heard about his pro-west statements he was exiled to Siberia.

   Woman: He will probably never get permission to live in Moscow again.

   ?   Where did the man want to work?

13. *Woman:* Why was Jimmy fired? He was such a good salesman.

   Man: You're right. In fact, he was one of our best salesmen but signing the petition is against company policy.

   ?   What happened to Jimmy?

14. *Man:*   Did Solzhenitsyn defect from the Soviet Union or did he emigrate from his country?

   Woman: Neither. His government just put him on a plane to Austria.

   ?   How did Solzhenitsyn leave his country?

15. *Woman:* I heard you are leaving for home tomorrow. How come?

   Man: I wanted to get an extension of stay but I guess I didn't go through the proper channels, and I received a notice that I must leave the country by Tuesday.

   ?   Why is the man going back to his country?

Appendix F
Answer Key

Answer Key

1. Conversation

I.		II.		III.		IV.		V.	
1.	a	1.	b,c	1.	b	1.	c	1.	from
2.	b	2.	b,c	2.	a	2.	b	2.	To
3.	a	3.	a,b	3.	a	3.	b	3.	up
4.	c	4.	a,c	4.	b	4.	b	4.	about
5.	c	5.	a,c	5.	—	5.	c	5.	to
6.	a	6.	a,b	6.	b		*	6.	into
7.	a	7.	a,c	7.	b	1.	b	7.	on
8.	c	8.	a,b	8.	—	2.	c	8.	up
9.	b	9.	a,c	9.	a	3.	b	9.	to
10.	a	10.	b,c	10.	a	4.	b	10.	across
11.	b	11.	b,c	11.	b	5.	a	11.	with
12.	c	12.	a,b	12.	b	6.	a	12.	up
13.	b	13.	a,c	13.	—	7.	a	13.	on
14.	a	14.	a,b	14.	b	8.	c	14.	ahead
						9.	b		
						10.	b		

2. Work

I.		II.		III.		IV.		V.	
1.	b	1.	a,b	1.	a	1.	b	1.	for
2.	c	2.	a,c	2.	b	2.	c	2.	by
3.	a	3.	b,c	3.	b	3.	a	3.	in
4.	a	4.	a,c	4.	b	4.	b	4.	into
5.	a	5.	a,c	5.	b	5.	b	5.	with
6.	b	6.	a,b	6.	a	6.	a	6.	for
7.	c	7.	b,c	7.	b	7.	c	7.	with
8.	a	8.	a,b	8.	a	8.	b	8.	down
9.	c	9.	a,b	9.	b	9.	c	9.	off
10.	a	10.	a,b	10.	b	10.	a	10.	into
11.	b	11.	b,c	11.	a	11.	b	11.	in
12.	c	12.	b,c	12.	b	12.	b	12.	on
13.	a	13.	a,b	13.	—	13.	c	13.	with
14.	c	14.	b,c	14.	b	14.	b	14.	out
15.	a	15.	a,b	15.	—	15.	b	15.	over
16.	c	16.	b,c	16.	a	16.	a	16.	up
17.	a	17.	a,c	17.	b	17.	c	17.	out
18.	a	18.	a,b	18.	a	18.	b	18.	up
19.	b	19.	b,c	19.	b	19.	b	19.	with
						20.	c	20.	at
								21.	off

3. Residence

I.		II.		III.		IV.		V.	
1.	b	1.	a,c	1.	a	1.	c	1.	up
2.	a	2.	a,c	2.	b	2.	b	2.	up
3.	a	3.	a,b	3.	b	3.	c	3.	across
4.	c	4.	a,c	4.	a	4.	b	4.	over
5.	c	5.	a,b	5.	b	5.	c	5.	out
6.	c	6.	b,c	6.	a	6.	b	6.	up
7.	a	7.	b,c	7.	b	7.	c	7.	up
8.	a	8.	a,b	8.	b	8.	b	8.	in
9.	a	9.	a,b	9.	a	9.	c	9.	with
10.	c	10.	a,c	10.	—	10.	a	10.	out
11.	a	11.	b,c	11.	b	11.	a	11.	of
12.	b	12.	a,b	12.	—	12.	b		
13.	b	13.	a,b	13.	a	13.	c		
14.	c	14.	a,c	14.	a	14.	b		
15.	a	15.	a,b	15.	b	15.	a		

4. Crime

I.		II.		III.		IV.		V.	
1.	b	1.	b,c	1.	b	1.	d	1.	down
2.	c	2.	a,c	2.	a	2.	b	2.	in
3.	a	3.	a,b	3.	a	3.	b	3.	around
4.	b	4.	a,b	4.	a	4.	c	4.	up
5.	c	5.	a,c	5.	b	5.	c	5.	off
6.	a	6.	a,b	6.	b	6.	a	6.	away
7.	b	7.	a,b	7.	a	7.	a	7.	up
8.	a	8.	a,c	8.	a	8.	a	8.	up
9.	a	9.	a,b	9.	b	9.	d	9.	to
10.	c	10.	b,c	10.	b	10.	b	10.	up
11.	b	11.	a,c	11.	b	11.	d	11.	on
12.	c	12.	b,c	12.	b	12.	b	12.	to
13.	a	13.	a,b	13.	b	13.	d	13.	of
14.	a	14.	a,c	14.	b	14.	b	14.	with
15.	a	15.	a,b	15.	b	15.	a	15.	of
16.	a	16.	a,b	16.	b			16.	to
17.	c	17.	a,b	17.	b			17.	behind
18.	a	18.	a,b	18.	b			18.	for
19.	c	19.	a,b	19.	—			19.	from

5. Love

I.		II.		III.		IV.		V.	
1.	g	1.	a,b	1.	a	1.	b	1.	fell in love with
2.	q	2.	a,c	2.	b	2.	a	2.	take my eyes off
3.	r	3.	b,c	3.	b	3.	a	3.	making a pass at
4.	h	4.	a,b	4.	b	4.	b	4.	living together
5.	l	5.	a,c	5.	—	5.	b	5.	get along with
6.	a	6.	a,b	6.	b		*	6.	flirt with

7. m	7. b,c	7. b	1. b	7. have an affair with
8. b	8. b,c	8. a	2. b	8. get together
9. c	9. a,b	9. b	3. b	9. am infatuated with
10. d	10. b,c	10. —	4. b	10. swept me off my feet
11. i	11. a,c	11. b	5. c	
12. j	12. b,c	12. b		
13. k	13. a,c	13. b		
14. f	14. a,c	14. b		
15. n	15. a,c	15. b		
16. p	16. a,c	16. a		
17. o	17. a,c	17. b		
18. e	18. a,b	18. b		

6. Fashion

I.		II.		III.		IV.		V.	
1.	c	1.	a,b	1.	a	1.	b	1.	with
2.	a	2.	a,c	2.	b	2.	c	2.	out
3.	a	3.	a,b	3.	b	3.	b	3.	together
4.	b	4.	b,c	4.	b	4.	b	4.	out
5.	a	5.	a,b	5.	a	5.	c	5.	in
6.	b	6.	a,b	6.	a	6.	c	6.	out
7.	a	7.	a,b	7.	b	7.	b	7.	on
8.	b	8.	a,b	8.	a	8.	c	8.	on
9.	c	9.	a,c	9.	a	9.	c	9.	up
10.	b	10.	b,c	10.	b	10.	b	10.	off
11.	c	11.	a,c	11.	—	11.	c	11.	up
12.	a	12.	a,c	12.	a	12.	b	12.	up
13.	c	13.	a,b	13.	—	13.	c	13.	up
14.	a	14.	a,c	14.	b	14.	b	14.	with
15.	b	15.	a,b	15.	b	15.	c	15.	with
16.	c	16.	a,c	16.	—			16.	in

7. Anger

I.		II.		III.		IV.		V.	
1.	a	1.	a,b	1.	a	1.	c	1.	with
2.	c	2.	a,c	2.	b	2.	b	2.	out
3.	b	3.	a,b	3.	b	3.	b	3.	on
4.	c	4.	b,c	4.	b	4.	a	4.	about
5.	b	5.	a,b	5.	b	5.	c	5.	up
6.	a	6.	a,c	6.	b	6.	c	6.	on
7.	b	7.	b,c	7.	a	7.	c	7.	about
8.	c	8.	a,c	8.	a	8.	c	8.	of
9.	a	9.	a,b	9.	b	9.	a	9.	in
10.	b	10.	a,c	10.	b	10.	b	10.	out
11.	a	11.	b,c	11.	b	11.	c	11.	like
12.	a	12.	a,c	12.	b	12.	a	12.	up
13.	a	13.	a,b	13.	—	13.	a	13.	for

14. a	14. a,b	14. a	14. c	14. down
15. c	15. b,c	15. b	15. b	15. over
16. b	16. a,b	16. a		16. out
17. c	17. b,c	17. b		17. to

8. Travel

1. c	II.	1. a,c	III.	1. b	IV.	1. b	V.	1. out
2. c		2. a,b		2. b		2. c		2. up
3. b		3. b,c		3. a		3. a		3. by
4. c		4. a,c		4. a		4. c		4. into
5. a		5. a,c		5. b		5. c		5. out
6. b		6. a,c		6. b		6. a		6. over
7. a		7, a,c		7. b		7. c		7. into
8. a		8. a,b		8. b		8. a		8. across
9. b		9. b,c		9. —		9. c		9. to
10. b		10. b,c		10. a		10. c		10. up
11. b		11. a,b		11. a				11. around
12. a		12. a,b		12. —				12. off
13. c		13. b,c		13. —				13. back
14. b		14. a,b		14. b				14. for
15. a		15. b,c		15. b				15. over
16. b		16. a,b		16. a				16. time

9. Take It Easy

I.	1. b	II.	1. a,b	III.	1. a	IV.	a. b	V.	1. by
	2. a		2. a,c		2. a		2. c		2. out
	3. b		3. a,c		3. —		3. b		3. up
	4. b		4. b,c		4. a		4. a		4. around
	5. c		5. a,b		5. a		5. c		5. in
	6. c		6. a,c		6. b		6. a		6. up
	7. a		7. a,b		7. a		7. a		7. through
	8. c		8. b,c		8. —		8. b		8. over
	9. c		9. a,b		9. b		9. b		9. in
	10. a		10. a,b		10. a		10. a		10. on
	11. a		11. a,c		11. a		11. c		11. on
	12. a		12. a,c		12. a		12. c		12. up
	13. b		13. a,b		13. a		13. a		13. easy

10. Immigration

I.	1. b	II.	1. a,b	III.	1. b	IV.	1. c	V.	1. to
	2. c		2. a,c		2. b		2. b		2. from
	3. a		3. b,c		3. b		3. b		3. under
	4. c		4. a,c		4. b		4. c		4. from
	5. a		5. b,c		5. b		5. c		5. on
	6. a		6. a,c		6. b		6. b		6. against
	7. c		7. a,b		7. b		7. a		7. to

8. c	8. b,c	8. a	8. b	8. from
9. b	9. a,b	9. b	9. a	9. off
10. a	10. a,b	10. b	10. b	10. through
11. c	11. b,c	11. a	11. c	11. for
12. a	12. a,c	12. b	12. c	12. forward
13. a	13. a,b	13. b	13. b	13. to
14. c	14. a,c	14. b	14. c	14. in
15. a	15. a,b	15. b	15. b	15. with
16. c	16. a,c	16. b		16. for
17. a	17. a,b	17. b		17. out

General Review Section

II. CONTRASTING IDIOMS

1. b	21. b		
2. a	22. b		
3. a	23. a		
4. b	24. b		
5. b	25. a		
6. a	26. b		
7. a	27. b		
8. a	28. a		
9. a	29. b		
10. b	30. b		
11. a	31. b		
12. a	32. a		
13. b	33. b		
14. a	34. a		
15. a	35. a		
16. b	36. b		
17. b	37. a		
18. a	38. a		
19. a	39. a		
20. b	40. a		
	41. a		
	42. a		

III. THEME ASSOCIATION

1. crime
2. crime
3. love
4. love
5. conversation
6. travel
7. residence
8. travel
9. love
10. residence
11. conversation
12. immigration
13. conversation
14. work
15. work
16. love
17. crime
18. love
19. love
20. anger

A CROSSWORD PUZZLE OF IDIOMS